All Night, All Day

Life, Death & Angels

All Night, All Day, is a gracefully executed anthology of hope, a merciful reminder we are not alone in this world. Each story, poem, and essay, a feather knitted upon an angel's wing.

—Robert Gwaltney, author of *The Cicada Tree*

In this stunning anthology which explores so many heartwarming brushes with celestial beings, all these angels are messengers come to assure us we are not alone and we are loved.

—Margaret McMullan, author of *Where the Angels Lived*

All Night, All Day is an anthology to be savored, beautifully exploring the themes of life, death and angels. Within this collection are remembrances and memorials, which pay homage to a loved one or to a mystical experience. Crafting an anthology is an art. Susan Cushman has done a big topic justice—the sum of the parts is greater for having been compiled together.

—Carol Van Den Hende, author of
Orchid Blooming and *Goodbye, Orchid*

These stories tell of unexpected humanity and love in the lives of those who needed affirmation of spirituality in the human world. The presence of angels was recounted through brilliant and descriptive imagery, and intriguing yet identifiable characterization.

—Francine Rodriquez, author of *A Woman's Story*

The reader is treated with a wide-range of storytelling and writing styles each pointing a way to introspection, restoration and healing. In the hush of a still night there is a soft beauty in the laughter and tears the reader will discover as love gently laps at the door of all the things we hold dear.

—Donna Keel Armer, author of *Solo in Salento: A Memoir*

All Night, All Day

Life, Death & Angels

Edited by Susan Cushman

MADVILLE
PUBLISHING

Lake Dallas, Texas

Printed in the United States of America

FIRST EDITION

Requests for permission to reprint material
from this work should be sent to:

Permissions
Madville Publishing
P.O. Box 358
Lake Dallas, TX 75065

Cover Design: Jacqueline V. Davis
Cover Art: "Rainbow Angel" by Nancy Anne Mardis

ISBN: 978-1-956440-45-4 paperback,
978-1-956440-46-1 ebook
Library of Congress Control Number: 2023930883

This collection is dedicated to my friend and mentor, Cassandra King Conroy, who inspired me to gather and share these beautiful pieces as we remembered together the angel that visited her home when her husband, Pat Conroy, was dying in 2016. Cassandra and Pat are my favorite authors.

Table of Contents

Friends

Foreword

Sophy Burnham

As one who has seen angels with her own eyes and written several books on angels, mystical experiences, and those extraordinary moments when the veil between the physical and spiritual world is pierced, as one who once had her life saved dramatically by an angel and who has given talks and led workshops around the world on the reality of the spiritual dimension, I am delighted to see an anthology brought out by a secular press. Does this mean that the search for God and trusting in the small, magical coincidences that offer meaning to life have moved into mainstream secular thought?

For many years merely to talk of angels invited scorn. Belief bespoke of craziness, even schizophrenia, and certainly denoted a pitiful lack of intellect. But after eight decades of personal observation, I fearlessly assert that angels are real. We swim like fish in spiritual waters, and like fish we know nothing of water until we're yanked out flopping and gasping on the grass. We're tossed back and swim away, confused—"Was that real? Did I really see what I think I saw?" We live in a universe of goodness, one that wants more and better for us than we can possibly imagine, and, when our spiritual eyes open, we find beauty, hope and courage, even in our suffering. Angels form only one small part of it.

I like to think most people know this deep in the well of our being. We have an experience. We don't mention it. But neither do we forget. We hold it to our hearts, for it is too precious, too sacred, to cast like pearls before other people's doubt. When my work, *A Book of Angels*, was published in 1990, the editors expected to sell only a few thousand copies. Yet somehow, with no marketing and no publicity, book stores could not keep it on their shelves. People bought ten and twelve copies ("It fell off the shelf at my feet") to give to their friends, who bought ten and twelve copies to give to theirs. It became a phenomenon, inspiring two or three hundred books a year on angels, followed by films and TV shows and stores devoted to angel items. Suddenly angels were everywhere. People had permission to tell their own stories. And they did.

What are angels? They are messengers. The very word comes from the Greek, meaning, "messenger," and the messages come in any way that they can be received. The question is, can we recognize them when they come?

Angels come disguised. They send their messages in dreams. They come as the little tap of intuition on your shoulder that whispers, "Go here, not there." (And we've all had that: we've all said, "I *knew* I shouldn't have gone that road, and I didn't listen!") They come as accidents and coincidences, inexplicable shifts of time and space, warp-speed incidents, always in our favor. Walking worried, you overhear the man waiting beside you on the curb say just what you needed to know. Out of the blue, a person you searched for telephones; or you meet a long-lost friend, impossibly, in a distant city to complete unfinished business. They come as animals—and I have wondrous stories of angels appearing as dogs. They come as other people; and, like angels everywhere, vanish never to be seen again. Sometimes, you yourself are used unwittingly as an angel to bring an important message to someone else. You may not even know you are doing it, until you meet a stranger, who thanks you for your help.

"What are you talking about?" you ask.

"Don't you remember? I was standing on Key Bridge when you passed and said, 'Good morning.' And I didn't jump."

Sometimes you are walking along, sunk in despair or sorrow, and suddenly, inexplicably, you are washed with joy. Brushed by an angel's wing.

And sometimes, rarely, the angels come in their own visible form. Then you are overwhelmed by love. They appear in such glory and beauty that you cannot believe it, but neither can you forget what you have seen, nor the unfathomable love, comfort, and meaning to life that they bestowed: the implacable knowledge that you are loved. You are loved beyond reason. You love. You are formed of love, and everything is shining with light—all the grasses, and trees, and dogs, and humans walk around enveloped in light. How is it you never saw before?

Carl Jung, the psychiatrist, was once interviewed by the BBC. "Do you believe in God?"

"I don't believe," he said. "I know."

The interview was reported the next day in *The London Times* but without the comma.

"Do you believe in God?" And the answer, "I don't believe I know."

Angels are different from ghosts or spirits of those who have passed over. Ghosts are seen as smoke, a will o' the wisp, and when a ghost passes or walks through you, you shudder with an Arctic cold. The spirit may be restless, concerned, lost, confused, or it may appear simply out of love. It may bring news or comfort, and often, especially after death, it comes to tell you they are all right. But an angel is different.

There are three marks of an angel. First it brings warmth, comfort, safety. "Home," you cry as your soul leaps out of your body, or, "Mother!"—the mother you wish you had had and that secretly you know in the tissues of your heart. An angel is the embodiment (if I may use a physical word) of love, for that's all an angel is, the heart of God.

Second, they always say the same thing: "Fear Not! Don't be afraid. We're here." They never say, "Well, you sure made a mess of things this time. Stupid girl!" There is never criticism, but only unfathomable love, support, power, comfort, safety, and even laughter. Joy!

Third, and perhaps most strangely, you cannot forget. Unlike most memories that fade with time, the experience of seeing an angel remains or even sharpens with time. Moreover, you are changed.

What do they look like? They may be male or female, or androgynous. With wings or without. They are cherub babies or bigger than a jumbo jet. They like disguise. If they come as a human, they blend unnoticed into their surroundings, and therefore wear something quirky or normal, a baseball cap. Or in one story, a cigarette dangles from their lips. They are tall or short, male or female. They come. In silence they perform their work. They vanish or disappear, or walk curiously away.

I have an entire file of the flat-tire angels. These happen mostly to women, it seems. You are driving down a lonely road when you have a flat. Just then a car pulls up and a youthful man gets out. Or two. Without speaking, they busily change the tire. They may murmur to one another, and though you can hear them you cannot quite catch or understand the words. Still, you feel no fear, but only a curious happiness and peace. They change the tire, get back in their car and drive away. Yet you never see them leave. If it's a curvy road, their car disappears appropriately behind a bend. But if it's a long, straight road, you are suddenly impelled to turn away for a second, and when you look back, the road is empty. How could the car have vanished so fast?

I mentioned angels that come as animals. Here's one: Late at night, a woman, tired from work, got on an empty bus to go home. At the next stop a frightening man got on, and she had that goose-bump, shiver of surety that he intended to follow her home. She began to pray. She lived on an unlighted, country road, and sure enough as she descended the bus at her stop, the man got off too. But just then a large, white, Great Newfoundland dog appeared out of nowhere, put his head under her hand, and walked beside her to her door, waited until she had the key in the latch, and trotted away. The man drifted off. The dog had never been seen before, and was never seen again.

Why do angels come sometimes and not at others? To women more than men? To children more than adults? What draws them to you? I think it is a vulnerable, childlike openness, and sense of wonder, the expectation of goodness. And of course they are pulled by prayer. I remember telling the group in one workshop that if they wanted to see their angel, they had only to ask. Ask it to show itself. But then you have to wait. Because the answer won't come on demand or how you expect. A few weeks later, one woman in the group wrote me that when she had gone back to Ohio, she decided to try. She settled at her meditation altar, and prayed and prayed to see her angel. Nothing happened. Finally, out of boredom and with some annoyance, she took the dogs for a walk in the nearby woods. There, she saw her husband's uncle coming toward her. Her heart sank; he always hit on her. To her surprise, however, this time he turned away, leaving her alone.

That night at a family party, he came up to her. "Who was that man you were walking with in the woods today?" he asked.

"What man?"

"You know," he insisted. "He must have been seven feet tall, walking to your right and a step behind you."

Oh, she thought! *My guardian angel! Just when I asked.*

You see what I mean about them not coming in the way you expect.

Does everyone have angels? Yes. We all have one or more angels who accompany us all throughout our lives. They watch over us at birth and carry us at death, for it's hard to be a human on this planet of suffering, a spiritual being having a physical experience. We need the angels to help us in this work. We need to remember, it's not that bad things don't happen to us. It's that when they do, we're not alone.

Angels can do anything. Angels can change all the physical laws of the universe—keep two cars from colliding, for example (and I have not one but two stories of cars that passed *through* each other without damage or harm to the startled occupants). They can warp time and shift space. But they cannot interfere with our free will. They can teach us, guard, warm, comfort, call for help, guide the surgeon's hand, deflect a dagger—but they cannot prevent the murderer from his intention, for he has free will.

As a student, my friend, Sarah, found herself in Greece one night on a lonely road so terrified by her isolated situation that she was paralyzed with fear. Unable to move. Almost fainting, she felt invisible hands behind her lift her up and carry her down the road. She was washed by light, love, warmth, comfort, safety, joy and peace. The being carried her across a bridge and dropped her. Falling, she skinned her knee—physical proof of the experience. She ran to the village, pounded up the steps to her pension, burst into the room she shared with other students. Her friends turned to her, "Sarah, what's happened?"

"Oh, nothing," she said, unwilling to tell of her terror or those strong hands.

"No," said one friend, approaching. "You are shining with light. You have seen God."

Years later she was raped. All during the attack she kept thinking, "Now my guardian angel will save me. Now my guardian angel will save me."

And no help came.

We talked about it a lot. I offered my reason—that they cannot interfere with our free will. But Sarah had a different idea: "No, I needed to learn to forgive more deeply," she said.

The stories in this anthology illustrate primarily those moments of illumination for which the angels are best known— their messages, their love; and many of them concern death. Is anything more important? Sometimes it is a grandfather who is the angel. Sometimes it is the author herself. Or her friend. The authors question faith, rebel against reality, shake their fists at God, fall to their knees, weep, laugh, smile in poignant remembrance, and all the while they are searching in humility and with grace for meaning to our lives. For forgiveness. For the ability to love more deeply. The courage to be lovers. To bear angelic messages, in this life.

Introduction

Three Beautiful Men and a Peacock
Susan Cushman

"Some angels are like peacocks. Others are less flashy. Like
city pigeons. It all depends on the wings."
—Shelley Pearsall, author of *Things Seen From Above*

I love peacocks. About twenty years ago, as I was studying
the ancient liturgical art of Byzantine iconography, I learned
that peacocks often appear in icons and other religious art as
symbols of rebirth, immortality, or resurrected life. This new
information was on my mind in 2005 when I was sitting with
my aunt in a hospice facility in Jackson, Mississippi. She was
nearing death from lung cancer, which had metastasized to her
brain. Barbara Jo was my father's younger sister. She had already
lost her husband (Dan), my father (Bill), and her other brother
(Jimmy Ray) to cancer.

At this stage of the disease she was in and out of consciousness, but she suddenly sat up in bed and pointed at the door to
her room, which was open, and said, "Oh, Susan! Look at that
beautiful peacock and those three beautiful men!"

Of course I got up and walked over to the door and looked
up and down the hall, but I didn't see any men or a peacock. I

sat back down beside Barbara Jo's bed and asked her who the three beautiful men were.

"They were Dan and Bill and Jimmy Ray!" I am certain she was seeing them in Heaven, where she would join them later that same day. And the peacock? He was assuring her of her own impending resurrection.

I have been blessed to be with four family members as they drew their last breath—Barbara Jo, my father, my mother, and my brother. There is something mystical about holding the hand of a person who is "crossing over." It can be heart breaking, of course, but also very holy and beautiful.

Some of the essays in this collection share the grief of personal loss when a loved one dies. Often the presence of an angel or another mystical experience is shared. And not just in death—there are also stories here of the way the mystical world interacts with us in daily life.

As Cassandra King shares in her essay, "Another Kind of Angel," a discussion we had at her house several years ago was the genesis of the idea for this book. I had read her memoir about life with her husband Pat Conroy, *Tell Me A Story*, and wanted to ask her more about the angel—or at least some believed it was an angel—who visited Pat and his family when he was near death. We both thought an anthology about angels and mystical experiences would be a good project. She immediately agreed to write an essay for the collection, although she remembered Pat's advice to her about not going over-board in her interest in the paranormal, and—as she says in her essay—"for God's sake don't *write* about it!" And yet, here we are, writing about it.

As I was inviting authors to contribute essays and short stories, I decided to include poetry. Poets really know how to get to the heart of things with their words, and I believe their contributions add another dimension to the book. I cast a wide net with the anthology's theme, inviting the writers to explore angels, end-of-life stories, and other mystical experiences. They came back with stories about all of the above, and their cast of (mostly non-fictional) characters includes—in addition to angels—mothers, fathers, sisters, grandfathers, friends, and even a homeless man and a dog.

About the title, which I struggled with for many weeks. Of course it takes us back to the African-American spiritual, "All Night, All Day," which Johnnie Bernhard writes about in her essay. I have found myself frequently humming, "angels watching over me," while working on this book.

While researching the topic of angels, I discovered Sophy Burnham, *New York Times* best-selling author of *The Book of Angels*. I was thrilled when Sophy agreed to write the Foreword for this wonderful collection. After reading her personal thoughts about angels, I decided to share a little of my own.

As a convert to Orthodox Christianity, I have found the Church's beliefs about angels to be fascinating. (As a side note, Frederica Mathewes-Green is also Orthodox, as she mentions in her essay, "A Choir of Angels.") The Orthodox teaching organizes these incorporeal beings into nine ranks, which are supported by Scripture: seraphim, cherubim, thrones, powers, dominions, authorities, principalities, archangels, and angels. We are taught that each of us receives a guardian angel at our baptism. And that there are seven archangels, five of whom appear in the Bible. Their purposes include the roles of messengers and guides for humans, as well as perpetually hymning God's glory.

So I invite you to open your heart and mind to the ways the spiritual world and its minions invade our earthly lives. As George Eliot said, "The golden moments in the stream of life rush past us and we see nothing but sand; the angels come to visit us, and we only know them when they are gone."

Mystics and Messengers

There are common themes, archetypal themes, in families.
This is the province of the medium: the dead want resolution, the medium assures us, of forgiveness, or peace. They
want us to know they are OK and they want us to take care
of ourselves, to find our own peace.

—Natasha Trethewey, "Clairvoyance," from *Memorial Drive*

Another Kind of Angel

Cassandra King

"For He will give His angels charge concerning you, to guard you in all your ways." *New American Standard Bible 1995*, Psalm 91:11

A couple of years ago I was enjoying a visit with my sister writer and dear friend, Susan Cushman, when the subject of angels came up. Not exactly your ordinary conversational topic, even for a couple of women like Susan and I, who share an interest in all things mystical. Everyone knows writers are "out there" anyway, prone to a fascination with anything weird and quirky. Whenever I mention my interest in the paranormal, my family tends to respond by exchanging glances behind my back and rolling their eyes. Even my former husband, a writer who had his own fascination with mystical experiences, cautioned me not go off the deep end. I'm not sure, but I think he was saying that exploring the possibilities is fine and dandy, but if you want to be taken seriously as a writer, make sure you don't stray beyond intellectual exploration. And for God's sake, don't *write* about it.

To the best of my recollection, that's how Susan and I got on the topic of angels. I'd recently published a memoir about my marriage to the late author Pat Conroy, and I told her about my misgivings in relating several strange occurrences surrounding his death. One was about a mysterious nurse, who might or might not have been an angel, and another about the appearance of a celestial bridge that seemed to transport my husband from this world to the next. When Susan seemed surprised that I'd had misgivings about relating the incidents in my memoir, I admitted to her that my hesitation had been foolish. After the book came out, I received an outpouring of mail from readers who wanted to tell me their stories of similar experiences during the death of a loved one. To my surprise, it was my story about the night nurse who might or might not have been an angel that they related to most. To my further surprise, I got as many messages from male readers as I did from female, which is unusual for a writer like me whose audience tends to be largely female. I could only surmise that the story had struck a chord with men who normally wouldn't feel comfortable talking about an encounter with an angel. And that's when I told Susan that she should consider collecting some of these stories, because the interest was definitely there.

To my knowledge, I've never had a personal encounter with a celestial being. Even with the night nurse, I was drifting in and out of sleep when it happened, and would've sworn it'd been a dream if others hadn't witnessed the same. But I've heard from plenty of others who have. The most vivid and mystifying encounter happened to my father, and his experience is seared in my memory. It is not a story I have shared often, mainly because I've felt that you had to know my father to appreciate the impact of his encounter.

I've written about Daddy before, not just in my memoir but also in various articles. He was quite a character, a great storyteller whose stories of growing up on a farm, coming of age during the Depression, adventures and misadventures serving in World War II fascinated his daughters (and later his grandchildren) just as much as his made-up tales of the ghosties and haints in the woods behind our house. Even so, Daddy always made the distinction between his true stories and the make-believe ones he told to entertain us—or to keep us from wandering in the swampy woods where true dangers lurked. So several years ago when he told my two sisters and me, in utter seriousness and shock, about his encounter with an angel, I never doubted that it happened, and exactly as he told it. Despite his skills as a raconteur, Daddy was a farmer of the old school, raised to honor the laws of nature. His livelihood depended on it. He might tell us a scary tale about a ghost who haunted the woods, but if you swore you'd seen it, he'd tell you there was no such thing. And if you persisted, he would laugh and tease you for being so gullible.

One of the King family's favorite and often-repeated stories had to do with angels, sort of, and was always good for a laugh. One bright summer morning we were sitting around the breakfast table when Daddy came in with the local newspaper, which he always picked up at the end of the driveway to read while he ate breakfast. It was a ritual of sorts, talking over breakfast about the goings-on of the community, farm prices, who'd gotten married or died, how the football games came out.

Between bites of his breakfast, Daddy read a full-page article in the religious section then burst into laughter. "Look at this," he said, and held up the picture for us to see. The article was about an occurrence at a little church just down the road from our farm. Quite close by, actually. It seems a miracle had caused an astonishing number of conversions. During a recent tent revival, angel feathers had floated down from the heavens to shower the congregation, who fell out in wonder like the shepherds of old, tending their flocks by night. The photograph showed the preacher holding up a handful of feathers, which could only be from heavenly beings because they were oddly shaped and pure white, unlike anything anyone had ever seen. "The Almighty has blessed us with a miracle of angel feathers," the preacher declared, "and many sinners have repented!"

Daddy made us promise we'd never tell anybody the truth

because of the backsliding bound to come about as a result. It looked like he'd be forced to build a pen for his new batch of guineas, he said, a unique white breed with unusual feathers. They tried to roost in the trees, but Daddy's blame bird dogs couldn't stop chasing them. The poor guineas squawked and flapped and sent their feathers flying everywhere. Just the other day, the dogs had chased the rare white guineas all the way to the road.

My father's encounter with an angel years later would be far from humorous, and to my knowledge, never shared with anyone but my sisters and me. It was 1992, and my mother, Pat (Pastine, but she'd always been Pat) planned a big celebration for her seventieth birthday that summer. It'd include a retirement party from the assisted-living home where she served as activities director. Mother was a robust dynamo of energy who'd never taken a sick day in all her years there. But lately she'd had some unexplained pain and her doctor had her in the hospital for tests. Nobody was worried, especially her doctor, who'd told her if all his patients were as healthy as her, he'd be out of business.

I was living in Birmingham at the time, teaching at a small college nearby, and had offered to come if she needed me. She wouldn't hear of it. My sister Beckie lived next door to her, and my other sister, Nancy Jane, only a few hours away. Late Friday afternoon I called Mother at the hospital to see if test results were in. We were on the phone when her doctor came in, and I heard him say, "Pat, it's cancer." My father repeated "Cancer?" in disbelief, and Mother said she'd call me back. No, I told her. I'll be there before visiting hours were over.

Traffic had been bad, and visiting hours had passed when I got to Mother's room. She'd sent Daddy home but my sisters had waited for me. We were worried but Mother was upbeat, which eased our fears. She insisted we go home to make sure Daddy got a good night's sleep. And for goodness sake, don't let him worry! She'd be just fine. They'd treat it and she'd be back to her old self.

Although in separate cars, Beckie, Nancy Jane, and I pulled into the house at the same time. After greeting Daddy's passel of dogs, we went in to find Daddy still up but in his pjs, waiting for us. Instead of hugs for Nancy Jane and me, neither of whom had been to visit in several weeks, he sat at his usual chair staring into space. When he turned to us, his face was a white as the proverbial sheet. And the expression was one I'd never seen before. It scared me.

"Daddy!" I gasped. "Are you okay?" I went over to put a hand on his shoulder. "I know you're worried, but Mother's fine. Really. You know how she is—she'll beat this. I promise you, she's going to be fine."

"No," he said as he shook his head. "She's not." Then he motioned toward the sofa. "You girls sit down. I need to tell you what happened."

Daddy turned to face the three of us on the sofa but his look was far away. In a daze, he stared somewhere beyond our line of sight. "I came home from the hospital and got ready for bed. I was worried about your mama—of course I was—but not scared or anything. Not as healthy as she is. If anybody could beat this, she could. I came in here and sat down to wait for y'all. Then I heard a knock on the door. Didn't make sense since I knew I hadn't locked it. I waited a minute and heard it again. Maybe somebody broke down on the road, I thought. So I went to the door."

He closed his eyes for a minute and rubbed his face before continuing with the story. "When I opened the door, my mama stood there."

Nancy Jane, sitting next to me, grabbed my hand, and I felt goosebumps sweep over me. My grandmother had died over thirty years ago. With that faraway look again, Daddy went on. "Mama had a dress she always wore to funerals, with a big black hat. It was pretty, not scary like it sounds. That's what she was wearing. But she wasn't a ghost, I swear. I saw her as plain as I see the three of y'all." He paused to look at us. "I said,

Mama—what are you doing here? And she said, I came for Pat. And then she was gone. She'd been there, right in front of me in her funeral dress, then she wasn't anymore. I was shaking but I went outside barefoot and looked all around. You know what got me? The dogs never barked. Don't nobody come here without them barking their fool heads off."

Nancy Jane jumped up and went to take Daddy's hand. The baby of the family and a daddy's girl, the two of them had a special bond. "You dreamed it, Daddy," she said emphatically. "You were in here waiting for us and you dozed off. That's all." He was shaking his head before she even finished.

"I don't blame you for not believing me," he said to her. "I wouldn't either, if somebody told me the same thing. But I know what I saw."

Beckie tried humor, which usually worked with Daddy. "Now, Daddy—you sure you didn't get into the Wild Turkey?"

He remained serious, shaking his head. "I haven't had a drop, and I was wide awake. It was my mama, is all I know. If I'd reached out I could've touched her. She came to prepare me. That'd be like Mama, wanting to help me see what was coming. She came to tell me that Pat wasn't going to make it, and I had to accept it."

He got to his feet and without even looking our way, said he was tired and going to bed. None of us knew what to say to him, so we just hugged him and told him to try to sleep. Before going down the hall, he glanced over his shoulder. "It was my mama," he said, then walked down the dark hall to his room.

Emotionally exhausted, my sisters and I decided to go to bed too so we could get to the hospital early. None of us knew what to think of our father's strange visitor, and we weren't ready to talk about it. Things would look different in the morning, we told ourselves.

I didn't think I'd sleep but did, hard. I'd forgotten to pull the curtains and the rising sun woke me. I got up and went to the double windows. The bedroom looked out over Daddy's fishpond, where he and Mother had a little cabin and spent so much happy time. As the sun turned the sky and pond water a startling shade of pink, the same color as the roses Mother had planted outside the windows, I realized my eyes were flooded with tears. That's odd, I thought. I'm not crying. As tears rolled down my cheeks, the whole scene blurred into a watery tableau of pink, and through it came the blinding rays of the sun. And something happened to me, something I might call mystical. My heart broke. It was a physical sensation, not painful but real in a way that few sensations are. And like my father after his encounter, I *knew*. With that knowing came grief but also a strange comfort. My breathing slowed, and I let the comfort in.

I wanted to go tell my sisters, to share the beautiful image and tell them how I was crying but I wasn't. I wanted to try to explain the peace that came over me, as though the watery scene was my sorrow and the rays of the sun the peace I'd been offered. But I didn't. Instead the image would imprint itself within me and carry me through my mother's death as well as many other losses to come. I left the bedroom and went to the breakfast table, where Daddy sat with his cup of coffee. Something told me he'd never mention the visit from his mother again. I put my hand on his and gave it a squeeze. "Daddy? It was your mama," I said. He didn't acknowledge my words, not then or ever. But I know he heard me.

Road Trip

Suzanne Henley

It was my turn. I stepped out of Weezie's Lexus and picked my way through the lot of crushed beer cans and tired weeds to the door of the double-wide. A toddler looked at me round-eyed from the other side of the screen. "Come on in, Hon," said a voice caressing a cigarette.

I discreetly held out my folded $15 and tried not to show my discomfort sitting across the small table as Juanita set her timer and shuffled the tarot cards. Two grandchildren wandered in and out of the room and hung over vinyl recliners with orange popsicles. Weezie had arranged this visit to the local psychic for each of us as part of our weekend in the small Georgia town of her childhood.

❧

The four of us—in our forties and early fifties—were all college- or graduate-school educated and responsible members of the community. My three friends had all been presidents of women's community organizations; we all served on community boards, voted regularly, and were committed parents—and active Episcopalians. Visiting a psychic was not part of our establishment lives. With each click of the odometer down the highway, however, we became at least subliminally aware of leaving our world of responsibilities—the years of parenting, marriage, and career—back home. Our parents were still healthy, and we were entering a creative sliver of time in between, a freedom when we'd discover and celebrate ourselves as individuals, sometimes even embracing new ideas that bucked the norm.

We stayed at Weezie's sister Rachel's stone house, built long ago by their grandmother Gamma—a legendary 4'11" redheaded firecracker, a community as well as family matriarch—down the large, wooded hill from her big house. Rachel had furnished and decorated the cottage with a swath of charm and taste, and she and her witty and generous personality alone were worth the trip. After all these years I can still hear her trademark, husky laugh. She was going through a difficult divorce and, although I don't really know, I sense we were there partly as respite and distraction. I also think some others of us needed our own respite from ghosts of our own too-busy lives that needed addressing. But we never stopped the banter and laughter. This was not a weekend for contemplation. That would come later.

Next morning after a lazy breakfast, we headed for the antique shops in a nearby town, a small town like many other Southern ones dying from population, retail, agricultural, and lifestyle entropy. Downtowns were becoming ghost towns and, pre-internet, turning storefronts into antique or "junque" shops to attract the tourist economy was not uncommon. We wove in and out of shop after shop, leaving a trail of chatter like breadcrumbs in our wake. I bought a large, heavy, antique-brass, Chinese rice cooker with a burnished patina that is still the coffee table in my living room. We stopped for ice cream at an old drugstore and drove around sightseeing, leaning out windows to wave at strangers. We carried on endless, competitive repartee. Impeccable timing, shared stories, one-liners, and punch lines were conversation traits we'd all been bottle-fed since birth as Southerners.

And then it was time for my appointment with Juanita.

Well, Juanita was a disappointment. She did not tell me I'd soon come into an unexpected fortune or meet the tall, dark, handsome love of my life and go on a cruise. After all these years, all I remember of her predictions was that I'd soon move into a trailer.

The irony of this humorously improbable prediction is that, four months later, I did.

As the project manager of a 1,000,000-light, drive-through holiday exhibit, one of my duties involved designing a trailer to accommodate the needs of hundreds of staff, volunteers, engineers, and ironworkers not only for the months of construction but for the days and nights of the two-month nightly exhibit. During the two-plus years I worked on this exhibit, I spent countless hours, rain and cold, day and night, in this trailer. Juanita was right. I not only moved into a trailer, I designed it from scratch.

৩

After our appointments we straggled back to Rachel's, chopping and cutting to help prepare dinner while emptying a really fine bottle of pinot noir. After dinner we carried our glasses to the living room fireplace, a crackling fire awaiting us against the night's chill. We plopped down willy nilly, leaning against each other's chair legs or arms, and spring-loaded our story-telling again. With each sip, each pop of a log, the sound of our laughter rose. And, gradually, with each swirl of the wine's deep red caught in the crystal glasses by the firelight, the wave of our voices dropped, as one or another shared some hesitant, personal story, the kind usually held close to the bone. For several beats, we'd stare into the fire and let our thoughts catch up with our stories.

We'd be leaving early the next morning and finally realized we needed to pack and go to bed. As we stood up and shook ourselves into shape, Rachel leaned back in her chair, looked up at us, and said, "Y'all know, before I got married, Gamma took me aside and told me my life would never be the same again. 'And,' she said, 'when that first baby comes, Rachel, you'll never ever have gal time again.'"

"After all these years, y'all, I feel like that's what this weekend and tonight have given me, a gift of 'gal time' once again. And, oh, I thank you."

We all hugged and said our good nights. Dorothy and I were sharing Gamma's old front bedroom. I pulled clothes out of my bag for the next morning, threw the two tortoise-shell side combs I wear in my hair on the top of the Victorian dresser, and fell into bed. I turned my back to Dorothy and didn't remember a thing 'til the next morning. Bacon cooking.

Everyone else was already up and dressed. Dorothy's vanity was an ornate desk and mirror perpendicular to the dresser I was using. Dressed, I started the laborious process of getting the brush through my long, thick, unruly hair. I carefully brushed out a handful of hair on the front right side of my head, pulled it up, arranged it in a slight swoop and held it in place with my left hand. Then, putting down my brush, I picked up one of the combs, and anchored it in my hair slightly toward the back on the right.

I picked up the brush again and brushed out a handful of hair on the left. After laying the brush down, I again arranged the swoop of hair the comb would hold, held it with my left hand, and reached down for the other comb.

There was no other comb.

I looked all over the mahogany vanity, patted the surface, and realized I had heard no sound or felt movement against my hand to have knocked it off the vanity. The rug was an Oriental, and I thought *well, maybe I can't see the comb because of the rug's pattern and colors.* Holding half my hair out of my face, I got down and patted over several feet of rug. No comb.

"Dorothy," I sighed, "what did you do with my comb?"

"Uh, nothing."

"This is really silly, but would you come over here and help me find it?"

After a thorough repeat of movements by us both, the comb was nowhere. Dorothy and I looked at each other and shrugged. There was nothing else to do. Dorothy went back to her make-up.

I knew I could pull out the one comb in my hair, pull back both sides of my hair, and the one comb would hold all of it back, so I tossed the comb down on the dresser top, brushed and rearranged a handful of hair on the top back of my head, and lay the brush down. I then reached to pick that comb back up again.

I reached out but, glancing down, I saw not one comb, but two, two combs. Carefully arranged smack in the middle of the dresser, aligned and symmetrical, the combs made a tight square, one comb above but touching the top of the other, as though someone were making an emphatic but playful point.

I was not aware of any thoughts or how long I stood there staring at them before I said, "Dorothy, Dorothy. Here." She walked around beside me, looked at the two combs, looked up expressionless, and walked out of the room into the bathroom, saying "I knew there was something going on in here" over her shoulder.

We went to tell everyone else. But rather than being excited about such an extraordinary event and wanting to hear the details again, they scoffed. Their reactions bewildered me. I, usually the skeptic, felt impatient. I was miffed. Then Dorothy and I asked Mimi, who'd been taking snapshots of the cottage's rooms and décor, to take a picture in our bedroom. Rachel mentioned that Mimi and Weezie's room was also part of the original cottage when Gamma was building the big house. So Mimi finished the roll of 24 prints taking shots of the two bedrooms.

We loaded the car, waved good-bye to Rachel, and began the drive down the winding incline. Settling into our seatbelts, we suddenly heard Rachel shrieking, running from the house towards us, legs racing and spraying gravel, arms wide, her kimono floating out like wings behind her. "I just remembered, y'all, I just remembered, I never ever once saw Gamma without combs in her hair!"

⌒⌣·⌣⌒

How ironic that it would be a plastic, fake-tortoise-shell hair comb made in China—not even a family heirloom of antique French tortoise—that pulled back the onion-skin-thin layer of a different universe for me to peek into, I, an unexceptional, garden-variety woman in the 1990s standing alone and unsuspecting on an early March-bright morning in a small bedroom in a small Georgia town after a night of "gal time."

This experience forever changed the axis of my universe. My vision has never been the same.

Running through my predictable days in Memphis—not even a geographical pin-prick in our galaxy—while dashing in to Kroger for fresh avocados, for instance, or stopping to fill the tank with gas, distracted by the minutiae of whatever a normal day is, I sometimes pause, reach up and touch one of my combs, briefly touch one to remind myself that it has pulled back not just my hair in an idle moment, but the curtain to a new dimension of our universe—a dimension that Dorothy and I did not read about as a theory in a book, but actually experienced—a larger world not defined by the linear realities we take for granted—and one that, thank heavens, has a sense of humor.

It is way beyond my paygrade to think about naming this experience. Contemporary categories of physics go rat-a-tat-tat through my head, but I do not begin to comprehend quantum mechanics, the fourth dimension, relativity, time and space warp, parallel universes. I do understand with great depth and gratitude, though, the concepts "humbling" and "joy." What an enormous gift to have been handed this experience, a hinge opening to the vastness of all that is holy.

No, I no longer roll my eyes the way I would have in my "smaller" world, but they do now occasionally fill with tears. In astonishment. And awe. And gratitude.

☙

Back in Memphis, when the prints from the trip were ready the next week, we met in a red-vinyl-padded booth at Walgreens. Mimi came back from the photo department and slowly laid out the prints one at a time on the Formica top, face-up, like tarot cards. The first twenty-two prints were razor-sharp and well lit. The last two, however, remain unexplained. A heavy, charcoal-gray veil seems thrown across both prints. Details in the room are indiscernible. A jagged flash of something bright seems stopped in mid-air across the middle of each.

Trouble Comes Around

River Jordan

[Ed. Note: This is a short story (fiction).]

He was an old man without mercy or regret. Lived to himself in a wood so thick with scrub-brush and undergrowth nobody saw his camper or his truck. He kept to himself, the only company he had left that he didn't argue with or have a mind to backhand on account of what they said was spittin' stupid.

There was a woman back there in his history he'd not take party with. That love affair had been insane from the start and nowhere to go but down, down, down. The most good sense he'd had was to get out of there while he still had time and that'd been fifty years ago now. And the second thing was not to procreate in a world he thought had gone to shit before he ever had a chance to say otherwise.

It was that kind of life. A way to live alone, to keep to himself and not let down his guard. He liked it that way. Didn't have to suffer fools, didn't have to keep himself up, let his beard grow to his waist and didn't give a damn. What felt good was not asking nobody's advice about nothing or heeding what they come up with on their own when their opinion had not been asked for at all.

It was summertime so he spent most of his days outside the camper and if he'd been a praying man he would have prayed for little things. A breeze, a rush of rain, a clear night sky, a shooting star. Things he could appreciate all by himself. But he kept the simple prayers to himself, having given up on the almighty a long time ago.

The morning God called his hand he had been same old as always, making coffee in the early morning hours before dawn. Watching the sun come up with that first good cup in his hand. The light getting stronger, the darkness fading away, him stepping into another day he could do as he damn well pleased. Live far enough back off the road, deep enough in the woods and you were satisfied with being out on your own, nothing to interfere.

An hour after sunrise he heard the voice of a girl. It perked him, made him listen stronger. Nothing came this way down his road. Was no account of a reason for anyone to as there was nothing down here but him and he was of no interest to nobody anymore. Hadn't been for many years.

"Get out of here," the voice called loud enough he could now make out the words. "Shoo, get back!"

He cocked his head sideways, listening.

"Please, go on now, get back!" Then the voice changed, became fevered with fear. "Lord, have mercy."

He picked up his coffee, a blue and white tin cup with rust on half the lip of it. Took a sip, swallowed, hung his head. Then with the coffee in hand, old overalls on, he started towards the yelling. He stepped through the trees, the light breaking through the dense overgrowth. The scrub pulled at his overalls, snagged, caught, and then he pulled away, kept pushing though till he got to the edge of the dirt road. Could see what was going on.

There was the girl, a young one from the looks of her and she was spouting off more words in a blue streak than he'd heard in a year.

"Hey, hey!" She had a large stick in her hand, was waving it in front of her and turning in small circles as she tried to shake the stick at three large, skinny dogs that circled her, their throats full of growls in what he knew was a formation that would go from stalkin' to killin' in no time. He had no words.

"Could you help me mister? I'm just trying to get home that all. Just out for a walk and trying to get back home. These dogs come up . . ." She quit speaking to him, then went back to shaking the stick while she pleaded, "Go on! Get back! Go on!"

What a young thing, too skinny to do much of anything for herself. Out numbered for sure and her out on these back roads where nobody come. He started to ask her, what are you doin'? Why you come down this road that's got no destination at the end? But his throat closed up on him. The dogs moved in closer, muzzles lowered, eyes on her.

Was a few moments in this world where the intersection of one thing and another is where all the balance hung. The difference between good and evil. The sweat of what has been, what will be. He felt a weight settle on his shoulders. He wiped his mouth with the back of his hand. Opened his mouth to speak, found his mouth too dry, took a sip of his coffee, tried again.

"Hey," the dogs paused their attack, rolled their eyes in his direction. Then something came upon him. Something that wasn't his to possess but it come to him anyway. It was an unction, a serious certainty, a power. He passed his coffee cup from his right hand to his left and with it raised his right arm like it was the arm of Moses at the Red Sea. "Hitonouttahere," he said with a rumbling voice that had been missing, hidden for years long gone.

Him and the girl watched the dogs as they yelled and took off like they'd be struck by lightning or feared the coming of it, all three of them disappearing into the dust of the hot summer morning and into the far away woods down the deserted road.

"Thank you, Lord have mercy! Thank you. I thought I was a goner."

She was a pretty girl. Had a nice smile and he could see well enough to see her hands shake as she tossed the stick off to the side into the woods. "Never had something like that happen. I mean sometimes a stray dog I could baby talk into submitting but those weren't like that. They wanted to kill me, you know?"

She stuck her hands in her back pockets, watched him for a few seconds and then asked him. "You do know that don't you? They were gonna kill me. I have no doubt about that."

He wanted to say some things to her. He wanted to tell her not to walk alone down dirt roads this far back. Not without a gun. Not without someone. He wanted to ask her why she walked alone and to tell her not to. He wanted to tell her he hoped she had someone who loved her, who'd be true, stay through the rough years to maybe what came next. The sweet love of older age. A kind of salvation. He wanted to ask her questions and tell her things. He took a sip of his coffee gone cold now and looked over the rim into her eyes. Then he turned without saying any of the things on his heart and walked slowly back through the growth.

"Hey!" she called, "where you going?" There was a pause while she waited in the space for him to answer but he just kept walking. "You're a freaking angel, you hear me? You're my angel! God sent you to save me."

Her voice grew fainter but she was yelling now so it rose anyway, made it to him.

"An angel I'm tellin' you! You saved me! You're my angel sure and true."

He paused for a minute, thought about turning around, about telling her that couldn't be so on account he was just a wasted up old man who hid from time but he kept a slow, steady pace through the woods to get back to his camper, his chair, his righteous life apart. Little by little the girl's voice grew fainter and he could tell she had taken up walking again, making her way back home and he hoped to a safe place in a good life.

That night, just before he fell asleep, he whispered, "I ain't nobody's angel." But then he remembered the power that had come upon him, the sureness in his raised arm that could have split the mightiest of waters wide open, revealed dry land. And as he drifted off into that place of other worlds he knew in a split moment on a summer morning, he'd been possessed by the hand of God and that was as close as he'd get to being an angel on this side of the veil and it was good enough for him. A smile on his grizzled face, he fell into a deep sleep possessed with the memory of love, the breath of forgiveness.

Letting Joy In

Sally Palmer Thomason

Journal Entry, July 29, 2021
Choosing to let in joy is a revolutionary act.
—Valarie Kaur, See No Stranger, Chapter 10.

Yesterday, July 28th, was his 92nd birthday but he was not here to celebrate. Seven months ago he died on Christmas Eve. And the hollow spot within me that fills with unexpected, near daily tears is very deep. I long for a visit, some indication from "the other side" that we are still connected. But he has not come.

I feel, and others have noted, ours was an exceptional partnership as we learned to live together for over six decades—slogging through a couple of deep emotional trenches and personal challenges, or skipping through the many, unique to us, delightful discoveries, extraordinary adventures and beautiful peaks—while admittedly, just plain stepping along through ordinary daily life. In our partnership/marriage of sixty-four and a half years we liked, as well as loved each other.

Over fifteen years ago, when our grandson was in high school, he declared he was coming to dinner on Wednesday nights and Wednesday nights became family dinner nights at our house. Yesterday was a Wednesday and as nine of us gathered for dinner and stood at our places around the table, my daughter asked me to say the blessing. I had not done my usual mental preparation, but as I asked for everyone to join hands, words came. Although I have no memory of those exact words, I felt his presence and a surge of joy—of love. Somehow, for a beautiful moment, joy blossomed in my heart.

Clairvoyance

Natasha Trethewey

Just weeks before her death, my mother visited a psychic for a reading. This is a detail I've never been able to let go. Beyond the transcripts of her phone conversations with Joel and the notes for a speech she wrote on a legal pad, it is one of the few clues I have about the contours of her last days. To enter that world, I have asked myself the same questions: *How was she going about her day-to-day life? What had she been thinking?*

I tell myself that I might find an answer through a kind of experiential research, that making my own visit to a psychic may reveal something useful in my attempt to reconstruct the events of May 1985. I want to know what she experienced in that hour with a medium, what she might have taken away from the encounter. Was she a skeptic, as I am? An agnostic willing to be convinced with evidence? What I do not admit to myself is that there is an undercurrent of desperation in my decision, that my visit to a medium might be more than simply academic, just as her visit might have been more than the entertainment she assured me it was back then.

My friend Cynthia knows a medium and offers to make an appointment for us to visit his apartment. I am willing to pay the $150 "just for the experience," I say, but I decide I don't want him to know anything about me. I tell her it is because of my skepticism, that I suspect he would use the internet to gather information before our meeting, so we agree that she will arrange the appointment, saying only that she'd like to bring a friend. As an added precaution, we agree also to give him a fake name when we meet: Cassandra. When the psychic opens the door at the appointed time, Cynthia introduces me as "Cassie."

The first thing I notice is his accent. He's a Brit, and offers to make us tea. He's making some for himself, and I read his offer as a way for him to learn some things about me, an attempt to get me chatting before the session begins. So I say very little, discussing the weather—already hot for early May—and sit down at the other side of his desk. The apartment seems new and sparsely decorated. There is a large computer monitor on the desk and I note that it is turned off, the screen dark. Cynthia sits to his right and a little behind him so he cannot see her face. I angle my body toward him and do not look at her. When we begin, I set my cell phone between us to record the conversation.

I've seen the performance of mediums on television, and our session begins in much the same way. He asks if two months mean anything to me, January and August. Often that is the moment someone in the audience or the person for whom the reading is being done will say, "Yes, that was my mother's birth month" or "That's when my father died." It provides a bit of a clue, a path the psychic might follow to try to extract more information in order to convince his subject that contact is being made. It is the first signal that the dead have supposedly emerged with messages for the living. The living—wanting so much to believe—unwittingly provide all the necessary information for the medium to guess some aspects of their lives and thus weave a story they want desperately to hear. It's a beautiful con. But I am determined to be unreadable, or readable only for misdirection, and to give him as little as possible, or nothing at all. I am hiding the reason I have come.

January and August. These are the birth months of Joel and

my brother, Joey. I think for a moment and decide to tell the medium this. "Yes, something's coming through," he says. "I don't know if they are still alive or not . . ." He pauses, his words trailing off. "They are," I say, adding nothing more. I watch him with a look of mild anticipation, as if to say, *And?* He has a yellow legal pad in front of him on which he begins jotting things down, dates and numbers, phrases that, he says, he is beginning to hear as the dead sidle up to him to speak. I am reading the medium, too, using what must be a similar methodology. He is perhaps in his late fifties or early sixties, white. His curly hair, worn on the longer side, is gray.

For the next half hour he tries various avenues to get information, to get me talking. He begins by asking if someone in my family had traveled a lot, perhaps in the military. I am almost fifty years old, and Cynthia is closer to sixty, and white. Looking at me, and the two of us together, he can assume that there is a good chance I am of an age that I might have a parent who was in the service—most likely during the Vietnam War. I decide to tell him that my father was in the navy—but I do not tell him the Canadian navy—and that he died in 2014. I do it to give him something easy, a line to follow in order to see what he will come up with, guessing. I do it so as not to reveal anything of why I am really there.

My whole life people have wondered "what" I am, what race or nationality. It is familiar to me, the way the medium is trying to figure out my origins. It's happened again and again: someone looking at me furtively, or calling me "exotic" and asking "What's your heritage?" Once, when I was making a purchase in a department store, the white salesman behind the counter was too nervous or too polite to ask—most likely not wanting to offend a white woman by assuming that she was anything but white. He needed to write, on the back of my check, the additional identifying information required back then: race and gender. Hesitating, his pen hovering he tried to look at me without my notice. I watched his face as he deliberated after a second and third glance at my features, my straight, fine hair, my skin color and clothing. He must have considered, too, how I had spoken and whether any of those factors matched his notions of certain people—black people. I stood there and said nothing as he scribbled the letters WF: the designation for white female. In the same week, with a different clerk, I had been given the designation BF. That time I had not been alone: I had been standing in line at the grocery store with a friend who is black. Now the medium is scribbling on his notepad, writing the letters NA. There are several ways the believer might seize upon that detail. In the moment, however, I am thinking only one designation of those letters, how he is writing the over and over: *Not Applicable. Not Applicable. Not Applicable.* As if nothing we are doing will bring me the answers I need.

It is necessary that I say something occasionally to keep the reading going, so I decide to tell him that, indeed, my father had sailed around the world—a reasonable assumption given his naval service—and the medium seems to be assuming that my father met my mother in one of those exotic places he traveled. Still, I can see that he canot guess my racial origins. My reticence leaves him with only guesswork, and the details he gets wrong serve only to harden my skepticism. I must be smirking a bit when he says that not only am I "very clever," but I "hide [my] thought processes well."

Another tactic: now he is writing the word *May.*

"I keep getting something about May," he says, "a name, someone in your family?"

"No," I say, shaking my head.

"May. May. I don't know—just think about it," he says. It is not a name of someone in my family. It is the month of May and he is shrewdly surmising the month must hold some significance for me since it is the very month I have come to see him. And of course, it does.

"Something is coming through, but it's a little distant and I'm having a hard time hearing. Sometimes they don't step close enough, but your father has. He wants you to know how proud he is of you."

When he tells me this, I can't stop the emotion welling up in my eyes. In my rational mind I know this is nothing the medium has ascertained from speaking with my father, but it is true nonetheless—and I knew it long before he died. I am quietly weeping only because my father has been gone just a few months and my grief is still fresh.

It's the response he's been waiting for. This, the medium must deduce, is why I have come. There are common themes, archetypal themes, in families. This is the province of the medium: the dead want resolution, the medium assures us, of forgiveness, or peace. They want us to know they are OK and they want us to take care of ourselves, to find out own peace.

There is a range of images and general questions a medium can pose to make one believe he has established contact: *Is there someone who died too soon? I'm getting a fedora, the smell of a cigar.* These are things that most likely any of us would have some connection to—no matter how tenuous. He goes with "Has anyone lost a leg?" I decide to give him this information—let him run with it. Why not? I am waiting for my mother to speak. My grandmother lost a leg. My mother's mother.

NA NA, he writes. I could tell him these are the first two letters of my name—to which he might reply that he was getting that, that someone was telling him. Or I could tell him that these letters spell the name I called my grandmother: Nana.

The medium does not know whether or not my mother is dead and has said very little about her. He tells me my father is quite present, boisterous, doing all the talking. Even if my mother were there, he implies—not knowing whether she is living or dead—my father is sucking all the air out of the underworld, doing all the talking, and only my grandmother has managed to get a word in.

"May," he says again, tilting his head as he looks at me. The gesture is a prompt for me to finally realize what I have been missing all along, to say, *Yes, of course!*—and still I don't. There is nothing left for him to do but wind down our session. "Your father is saying you need to take care of yourself," he tells me. "He's saying you'll want to come back and do this again, you'll *need* to."

When we leave I try to hide what I am thinking from Cynthia by talking only about how wrong the medium was, how hard he tried to figure out my race and why I was there. I didn't tell her that for all my over display of skepticism I would have given anything for a message from my mother, that I wanted more than anything for the medium's claims to make contact with the dead to be real.

Instead, I have only two options: to believe he was a fraud, or to believe that, after all these years, my mother would not emerge to communicate with me: that she'd have nothing to say.

I wait until I forget most of what the medium and I discussed before I listen to the recording of our session. I wait, in fact, two years, carrying the record of our conversation around with me on my phone under the title "Medium" with the date below it and the time it took: 5-6-2015; 1:22:46. When I walked out of his apartment, I knew that I wanted to experience it all over again, for research, convinced that the distance would make me even more dismissive of the whole enterprise. I'm smug when I touch the Play button on the phone, smug through nearly the entire session. Then I hear it, what he'd been saying over and over two years earlier: May. May. May. "Yes it was May, the month before her death, the fifth month of the year," I say out loud, watching as the timer on my phone winds down the minutes. That when it hits me; he's a Brit and so if I write the date numerically, as he might, in his calendar of appointments, it would appear like this: day first, then month: 6-5-2015. American would read that as June 5, which is the date of the thirtieth anniversary of my mother's death. It hits me so hard I weep.

Had I been so resistant that I didn't make room for her to speak? Had she found another way to let me know she was there?

Numerology is a kind of faith, a belief in the mystical relationship between numbers and events. Visiting the medium, I had held out only the most remote hope that my mother would speak through him, and even barely admitted *that* to myself. I had never imagined that I might find meaning in numbers instead. But now I see that I've always been obsessed with numbers, both as portents and as a way to make sense of my past—to see the patterns they reveal, etched like constellations discernible only in the clearest night sky.

I have long held fast to the idea that my story is written in my stars: that there was a pattern in place for me beginning with my birth, a child of an interracial marriage, on Confederate Memorial Day, exactly one hundred years to the day, April 26, that it was first celebrated in Mississippi: pattern in that the only birthday of my mother's I recall celebrating was her twenty-sixth, when I decorated a cake in the shape of a halved watermelon, twenty-six black seeds marking her time; in that I marked my own twenty-sixth birthday with melancholia, knowing it was the first time I'd reached an age I was vividly aware that my mother had been; that the year we moved to Atlanta, 1972, was the same year that the Confederate monument on Stone Mountain was finally completed; that my name means "resurrection" in Greek and that I have had now what I think of as a second Jesus year, counting down the thirty-three years it's been since her death—my whole adult life without her. Before and after. And now that I have reached this second Jesus year at age fifty-two, which of course is twenty-six doubled.

Irrational as it sounds, I have clung to the pattern these numbers make so as to bring order to the chaos over which I desperately need to believe I have control—or, at least, that I have the power to recognize, just as the ancients looked to the sky and saw the myths they live by writ large.

My rational mind knows very well what my irrational mind is doing. So why not let both exist simultaneously? This is, after all how I make metaphor. And it is how I find myself weeping with joy, suddenly, because I have found a way to believe, at last, that this was a sign: 6-5-2015, the simple reversal of the numbers to reflect the date as the British medium might have recorded it, evidence that my mother was indeed present during my session with him.

I am weeping with joy but the feeling is short-lived. When my rational mind takes over again, I am left only with a profound sense of absence: that, whether she had been there or not, she still had no words for me. Soon, I am weeping only at my own foolishness, my desperation.

Angels Watching Over Me

Signs an angel is nearby: finding a coin or a white feather; the unexpected appearance of a light breeze or a wing-shaped cloud; flickering lights; a cat or baby cocking its head at an unseen object; the sound of chanting or bells; a surge of warmth in the chest; a tingling sensation in the gut; a distinctive scent—often spicy for guardian angels, and floral for archangels.

—Sonja Livingston, "The Angels' Share"

*But God still sends them, these angels,
and they still go, doing what they can, even
as we pray one thing and do another. Over and over.
If they truly had halos, we would make them spin.*

—Jacqueline Allen Trimble, "The Truth About Angels"

The Angels' Share

Sonja Livingston

I. I knew the psychic had conjured family when the messages from the Great Beyond became unkind.

"Now *I* think you look fine," the medium whispered. "But your spirit guide is suggesting more exercise and green vegetables—maybe some better shoes."

My feet were pushed into a flimsy pair of flip flops. It was summer, about ten years ago, and I'd come to Lily Dale Assembly with friends to visit mediums and attend the famous spirit-channeling sessions in the woods. My heart thumped as those around me received messages. A spirit with an eagle tattoo hummed "Danny Boy." "My husband," an old woman sobbed. A spirit with a slight limp carried an oil-stained rag and warned his nephew to check his tire pressure before heading back to Buffalo. A gardening-inclined ghost told her daughter the roses out back are getting ready to bloom. These spirits sure are generous, I thought. Until it was my turn and my spirit did not bother with niceties before railing against the pudge of my body and wholly inadequate footwear.

"I'm only the channel," the medium's smile was strained by the delicate business of brokering conversations between the living and the dead. My small group had left the public session in the woods by then and five of us sat in the front room of the spiritualist's cottage—an enclosed porch of sorts, complete with wicker chairs and floral pillows. A soft place, and softness is what I wished for just then—a spirit who floated around in gossamer and limited her advice to air pressure and gardening tips.

"I'm getting a Native American vibe," the medium looked at me with a raised brow. "Does this sound like anyone you know?"

"My grandmother." I said, though it was the thick fog of disapproval that had settled into the room and not her lifetime claim of Mohawk blood that gave her away. "I guess you've channeled Anna Mae."

II. Lailah is the original guardian angel as far as I can tell. According to Jewish lore, it's Lailah's job to lead souls from Eden into the human womb and pour secrets into our ears as our bodies unfold from a rosette of cells. Lailah reveals what she knows about God, the future and all of human history—filling us with so much wisdom, our bodies glow like candles. Until right before birth, when Lailah taps our upper lip with a finger and wipes memory away, leaving us to come into this world clean and seeking—and with a fleshy divot between mouth and nose. Who knows why an angel gives and takes like this? We can't go through the world with borrowed light, I suppose. We must stumble and fall while finding wisdom of our own. But Lailah doesn't wholly abandon us. She hovers nearby as we flail about, watching as our fingers return to the place where she tapped us—the philtrum, it's called—and the finger instinctively returns to its soft landing when we struggle to recall something we once knew.

III. I saw my grandmother only four times in my life. The first time her husband pulled his false teeth from the cup in which they'd been soaking and chased my sister with them, biting Alicia so hard with his dentures, the skin on her upper arm turned red. On the plus side, we got to swing from a thick branch of the weeping willow out back. A few years later, Anna Mae dropped off a dress she'd made for Alicia's First Communion along with a generous helping of disdain. My grandmother didn't think much of my mother's brood of fatherless children. Anna Mae was no role model when it came to parenting but at least her kids all came from the same man. Such may have been her thinking as she swooped in with her white lace dress and razor-sharp words.

She visited again when I was in 2nd grade. She'd traded her sewing needles for cactus needles by then. The place she lived was called Needles, in fact—a forgotten corner of California surrounded by prickly plants and armored creatures scurrying along the desert floor. My mother was pregnant again, with no boyfriend or husband in sight. How she survived my grandmother's barbs, I do not know. I only remember the shell bracelets Anna Mae brought and the batch of silver dollars she sent from her winnings at slots later that same year.

I was a teenager when my grandmother appeared for the last time. She had a black eye. *From a bar fight*, she proclaimed, and because her drinking was the most solid thing about her, no one questioned whether a stranger had actually socked our grandmother or whether it was her husband's handiwork. Later that year, the two would sit opposite each other with shotguns pointed at the other's head. *Go on*, they'd goad, cradling their respective guns until they nodded off. I can see them, two overgrown briny children whose fighting was the only way they knew to touch. But my mother relayed this scene after Anna Mae's final visit, and my most lasting memory of my grandmother is the steak she bought, which cost more than any single food item we'd ever had, and which she used to nurse her black eye before telling my mother to salt it and fry it up.

IV. Signs an angel is nearby: finding a coin or a white feather; the unexpected appearance of a light breeze or a wing-shaped cloud; flickering lights; a cat or baby cocking its head at an unseen object; the sound of chanting or bells; a surge of warmth in the chest; a tingling sensation in the gut; a distinctive scent—often spicy for guardian angels, and floral for archangels. Since Anna Mae seems to be my angel, I pay no mind to coins or clouds and listen instead for the sound of cursing from on high.

V. I have no picture of Anna Mae as a kid so I must make one of my own. An angular girl leans beside a barrel, her face resting against the bent staves. It's 1930, in upper Vermont. Prohibition means men ferment mash in old tubs and makeshift stills or make runs to the Canadian border for rum and gin. Anna Mae cozies up to her barrel like other girls cozy up to pets, waiting for the portion of whiskey that escapes through the pores—the angels' share, it's called and the girl smiles as she inhales the fumes. She's eleven, her dark curls side-parted and cut to the chin. She wears a sky-blue frock with fluttery sleeves. There's no money for dresses but she learned to cook and clean as a small girl and her sewing is a point of pride. She must have found a bolt of fabric and made herself a dress. Her breasts have just started to bud and she cinches the waist to approximate the shape of a woman as she totters around in a pair of her mother's shoes. Irish grandmothers lend an impishness to her face, a sort of inherited twinkle to the eyes, which misleads because, by age eleven, Anna Mae is already more prickers than roses.

VI. If Heaven is anything like the movies and angels must earn their wings with good deeds, my grandmother will remain forever grounded. Anna Mae liked to look good and learned to dress stylishly, even as the world around her came undone, but I can't see her succumbing to the fuss of halos and flowing robes. I can't imagine her bearing a lantern to light anyone's path or flying in to save anyone from snakebite, like the angel I once read about in *Reader's Digest*.

How can someone be something in death she could not be in life?

My grandmother did not hug us. She did not read to us or bake cookies. She never called us *honey*, *darling*, or *sweetie-pie* and neither did we call her *Granny*, *Nana* or even *Grandma*. "The grandmother," we said, inserting a definite article to keep Anna Mae at arm's length. "The grandmother is on the phone drunk again from California," we'd report, as if she was playing a part that had little to do with us. "The grandmother called Father Callan again," we'd say when we learned she'd started phoning our parish priest from clear across the country. "The grandmother has died," we'd eventually whisper, feeling bad about nothing so much as how little we felt at all.

VII. Another picture of Anna Mae in my mind's eye, earlier than the last:

It's 1926 and Anna Mae has just turned seven. The baby is another chore, but at four months old, her newest sister might just be the prettiest thing she's ever seen. With her two brothers, aged three and five, and Dot just a year old, the house was full before little Ellen came along. All those mouths and never enough food. The Depression that's about to seize the nation has held Anna Mae's family between its teeth for years. Is there any poverty like rural New England poverty? Frozen rivers. Chipped paint. Everything brittle and pinched. The boys run ragged and hollering. *Stop that nonsense*, Anna Mae shouts. Dot's diaper needs changing and the baby's wailing again. She's maybe forty pounds, but Anna Mae tries to hold it all together. Tiny mother. Busy bee. Where are the adults? Working perhaps. Visiting family. Passed out from the latest trip to the border for booze. The baby's crying is garbled now. Anna Mae scours the cupboard, running her hands along the shelves, as if a sack of potatoes and a single onion might appear in spaces that were empty seconds before. She's a clever girl and might try to make a mash of water and flour while praying for her mother to arise as the baby's face goes from pink to red to blue.

Lack of Care is listed as the official cause of death.

Malnutrition is a contributing factor.

Does Anna Mae ever forgive herself for living? What does it mean to live anyway? The question itself is precious. *To live means to stand upright,* I hear my grandmother answer. *To blink your eyes, to breathe, to piss.* But there's something else to living, isn't there? Another thing, clean as wood sap, soft as baby's skin, pretty as a sky-blue dress—but harder to see. Anna Mae might know this but cannot reach it, which is why she lets the whiskey burn a path to the gut where it puts the devil to sleep.

VIII. I wonder why my grandmother, who'd stopped going to church years before, called our priest several times in the year before she died. She was drunk when she called, we knew, but the priest never revealed the subject of her sloshy calls. Probably she wanted him to understand the extent of my mother's inadequacies and our illegitimacy before he welcomed us to communion on Sundays. Maybe she shared her grand scheme of going up to the border and the St. Regis Reservation to demand a portion of her ancestral land. Another possibility, however unlikely, is that Anna Mae found the priest as shockingly gentle as we did and spoke of things long ago tucked away. Maybe she made a confession in the months before she died—telling the young priest about the darkness of certain rooms in winter, the pile of things in need of doing for her baby sister, the way she'd checked and rechecked that cupboard, but still believes she might have done more, saying how—even after all these years—drinking is the only thing that washes the sound of crying away.

IX. Anna Mae is seventeen when she launches her first escape. She may look west from the Connecticut River toward the Green Mountains and beyond, to the crumbling Fort at Ticonderoga where she was born and the Adirondacks rising blue and purple in the distance. But the man she marries cuts down trees for a living and the logging camps are east, so they settle into New Hampshire's Presidential Range. She'll have a child two months after her wedding day and be pregnant again by the following summer, making the freedom she sought from the care and keeping of others look less likely every year.

One day, she'll take off altogether, leaving the woodcutter and her children behind. One day, my mother will do the same. But first, Anna Mae sews clothes for her children, bakes pies and takes my mother with her to Mass. They'll cross themselves and say prayers but leave little room in their lives for angels or other soft and beautiful things. Strange to come from a line of women who make an art of flight but do not let themselves believe in wings.

X. Though we rarely saw her, Anna Mae's mark was always felt. Her particular absence, and the much larger absence of grandmotherly affection shaped our lives as much as anything else. How small my mother seemed when filtered through her own mother's eyes, how lasting Anna Mae's needling voice, how persistent this inheritance of distance, abandonment and flight. Near or far, it does not matter. Anna Mae is the cloth we were cut from, fashioned and stitched.

The arrival of a cantankerous spirit wasn't the outcome I'd hoped for back when I'd visited Lily Dale with friends, but how much more disappointing would it have been if the psychic had sifted the air with the net of her conjuring head and came up empty? Which is worse, a terrible angel or no angel at all?

XI. After all these years and all this thinking, I'm not sure I've figured out the difference between angels and devils and ordinary human beings. What's left to do but close my eyes and fly west until I find Anna Mae asleep in her chair holding her shotgun like a love? Where else to go but Needles, California, where the clatter of cactus wrens has died down and nightjars sail open-mouthed over the cooling desert floor? And since I'm here, why not pick up the empty bottles and overturned cups before teasing the gun from my grandmother's hands?

I pull a blanket the color of sunset up to her chin and trace the ridge of her shoulder blade to feel for the place where wings might grow. And just like that, all the secrets I once knew return like the swath of stars just out the window, so bright the scorpions glow under the shimmering field of light. *What if my job is learning to make feather of needle and bone*, I wonder while considering the wisdom Lailah lavished then took away. *What if Anna Mae's job is to teach me this trick?*

How I'd like to shake Anna Mae awake and share the thoughts flooding my head. "What if angels are like the mist coming off Lake Champlain in late August," I want to ask. "Like the cactus that opens its white petals at night?"

And while I understand that this visit to my grandmother is powered by longing and imagination, I find myself closer to her than ever before.

"What if angels are like Jonah praying in the belly of the whale," I whisper. "Like Gabriel visiting Mary when no one else can see—not untrue so much as hidden beneath the hard seams of the given world?"

Angels Watching Over Me

Johnnie Bernhard

Many years ago, I attended a church retreat with my sisters in Palacios, Texas. Palacios is located along the Tres Palacios Bay, an inland bay of Matagorda Bay, on the central coast of Texas. Like most of the small towns along the Texas coast, it is culturally diverse and poor. The water is mud brown, mosquitoes outnumber sea gulls, and hurricanes wreak havoc from July to November. But we loved our summer pilgrimage to the outpost on the Gulf Coast. We celebrated the last day of school knowing the endless days of summer would soon begin in Palacios.

Summertime was a visual of little girls wearing shorts and tennis shoes in the hot humid mornings, streaking through the leaded windows of the former army barracks we slept in at camp. The juxtaposition of holding a youth spiritual retreat at a facility serving as a WWII training base—as well as housing for German prisoners of war—was lost on the young campers. I'm sure my mother knew. She had a sixth sense for places where people suffered.

I loved staying in the dorms, despite their history. What made those old bunk beds, scratched wooden floors, and drab white walls special were all the little girls tucked into those rooms at night. Smelling of Jergens Lotion and talcum powder, we'd lie awake, arms crossed behind our heads, whispering to each other about what happened that day or what we couldn't wait to do the next day. Occasionally, a riotous laugh interrupted the whispering, causing the camp counselors, our mothers, to shine multiple flashlights in the direction of the troublemaker. After various threats of a daybreak roll call, the flashlights were turned off. And like magic, little girl by little girl, we whispered our good nights, until the one girl, and there always was that one girl, sang out in the darkness, "And don't let the bed bugs bite!" Again, the communal laughter, again the hushing from the adults, until one by one, we fell asleep.

I learned many things during the week at the retreat. Every day there was a parable read from the Gospel. Every day there was an art project with pipe cleaners and glitter. Every day there was a new song to learn during the power hour of praise. I'm not certain that was what the specific time in the schedule was called, but it felt like an electrical surge of power when I sang my heart out with other little girls.

One summer we learned a song that I later discovered was an African spiritual. I've never forgotten the beauty of the lyrics and its joyful profession of faith. It has served me well throughout my life, especially during difficult times: "All night, all day, angels watching over me, my Lord. All night, all day, angels watching over me. Pray the Lord my soul to keep, angels watching over me."

My sisters and I believed without reserve, as only children can do, angels existed. I grew up in a home where visitations from angels and entrapments of the devil created a world of good versus evil. As an adult, I realized the world was often a blending of the two extremes. Bad things happened to good people. Hearts were broken with little regard. But I also learned in the hours of a church retreat that faith and love always prevail. Every faith lesson learned through the years was based on the words of Christ, "Love one another."

I wish I had always readily given my love to others. Those regrets never soften with time. They became the reasons I studied the saints and angels as extraordinary examples of love. The more I read, the more I realized the truth behind our inability to love unconditionally. Fragile egos buried in fearful hearts build impenetrable walls. Becoming fully human, the loving beings we were created to be, may be our life's most important journey. My journey began within my family–our idiosyncrasies and our faith.

I came from a family of story tellers based on our habit of sharing our dreams from the night before and discussing them with coffee in the morning. The telling of the dream was set like a plot. There was a setting, rich in color and sensory details, along with the characters, who came from our conscious lives, or angels with a message. Interpreting that message was the topic throughout the day—what did the dream mean?

It wasn't until I attended college that I realized most families don't talk about their dreams. College was the first institution where my beliefs were challenged. It was the first time I lived within a community other than my family.

After side glances and smirks from roommates and boyfriends, I began to question my family's idiosyncrasies, dream interpretations and visiting angels. I decided rejection from my peers was not nearly as painful as losing the hope an angel protected me.

For my family, the interpretation of dreams and angels was always set in the spiritual. Today, I realize those long-ago reflections of dreams made me aware there was a presence beyond what I could physically see. Some things I may never understand or be able to explain. I've always accepted that as a profound truth in life.

Hanging on the wall of the childhood bedroom I shared with my sister was a large framed print of an angel. The angel's wings grazed the shoulders of two small children walking across a bridge above a treacherous ravine. Lying in the dark with my sister next to me, I was comforted by the picture for many years. I can't remember talking to my sister about it, but

I knew everyone around me felt the same, as children in their innocence so often do.

Years later I found the same print in a second hand store. The picture of the guardian angel and two children was originally painted by Hans Zatzka of the Academy of Fine Arts of Vienna, 1877-1882. He painted under the pseudonym H. Zabateri. I never learned the reason why he felt he could not use his given name on his work. Perhaps some political leader felt the need to crush people's core beliefs and any reflection of those beliefs into nihility.

I bought Mr. Zabateri's print and hung it in my first child's room near his crib, all the while singing a song I learned so long ago: "All night, all day, angels watching over me, my Lord."

⁐

I met an angel on a Southwest Airlines flight from Tampa to Houston twenty-one years ago. Two decades later, I remember the day and how he appeared. There was never a doubt in my mind he was an angel sent to help me on a sad day.

The call came early in the morning. My mother was being transported by ambulance to M.D. Anderson Hospital. There was nothing the oncologist at the local hospital could do for her. The finality of that decision began the family's trek to Houston. For the flight, I packed an overnight bag and a paperback copy of Faulkner's *As I Lay Dying*. I should have left that book behind. Not that it wasn't the work of a genius set in the angst of the Deep South with its theme of mortality; it was the family's painful trek, coinciding with mine, that broke my heart. I cried into my bag of peanuts. I cried through multiple cocktail napkins. I cried shamelessly until the kind stranger sitting next to me asked, "Is there anything I can do to help?"

He was a middle-aged Hispanic man, handsome and soft spoken. Perhaps it was knowing I'd never see this stranger again that created the intimacy between us, or it could have been the lack of judgment I saw in his eyes, but I told my story like a confession.

I also told him I needed help finding my sister, eight months pregnant with her first child, once we landed in Houston. I was overwhelmed by the fear of not finding her.

When we landed at Hobby Airport, it was a sea of people, scrambling to get their bags and themselves out of the airport as fast as they could. My new friend pointed out a young, very pregnant woman near the baggage claim area. I walked toward my sister, who hugged me, as we cried for the vulnerable little girls we had become, knowing our mother was dying. Suddenly, I remembered my friend standing next to me. I broke from my sister's embrace to introduce him, but he wasn't there. He simply vanished. I even walked around the area, searching for him, explaining to my sister who this man was and why she had to meet him. It then occurred to me I never asked him his name. He never asked me mine. I couldn't even describe the clothes he was wearing. I never saw him again. I never had the chance to thank him.

"All night, all day, angels watching over me, my Lord."

❧

I knew a woman from Louisiana who believed in an avenging angel. We worked for the same school system in St. Mary Parish in the early Nineties. She embraced the mysticism of the Catholic Church, a belief similar to the magical realism of a Gabriel García Márquez novel.

Barbara was an elementary teacher at a school located near the levees on the Atchafalaya River. The student population was poor. The school grounds portrayed the harshness of the students' lives with no landscaping, few sidewalks, and even fewer bicycles locked at the bike rack in front of the ancient building. Barbara was a woman who didn't have to work. She worked because she loved teaching children. It wasn't unusual for her to pay for dental work, healthcare, and groceries for her students and their families. She didn't tell me; a mutual friend did.

The only story Barbara shared with me about her students was the day she called upon her avenging angel to protect a child from being moved into the state foster care system. A case worker from the Louisiana Department of Children and Family Services was investigating the mother. Barbara didn't think poverty was a crime, nor was being a single parent. Her avenging angel silenced the case worker with a sore throat and a fever. Either she feared Barbara or the onslaught of the angel, but that case worker never returned. I was frightened by this story, believing every word of it. Who was I to think I understood the mysteries of faith?

I asked Barbara if I could pray with her at a grotto she visited once a month near Bayou Pigeon, a French speaking community of fishermen and plant workers. She considered it for some time, but she never invited me. She might have thought I was more curious, than faithful. I never doubted Barbara's faith as something private and sacred. Her avenging angel was a gift, not a circus act.

"All night, all day, angels watching over me, my Lord."

⌒⋯⌒

My grandmother told me God sends other messengers to us, besides angels. Born at the turn of the Twentieth Century, she knew tremendous hardships during her lifetime—world wars, the Great Depression, hurricanes, and personal loss. She had an unbreakable spirit with an unquestionable faith.

I spent much of my early childhood in my grandparents' home. They began each morning sitting at a large wooden table in the kitchen, drinking coffee and reading their Bibles. The morning ritual was just that, a ritual practiced in privacy, never for public display or praise. It was simply a part of their daily lives, like brushing their teeth and combing their hair.

An artist, Grandma worked mostly in oils, capturing her

love of the bucolic life she lived in paintings of flowers, trees, and birds. She was fond of cardinals, especially the male with his bright red coat. Every time we saw one, she'd say to me someone in Heaven was thinking about us. The perky red bird was God's special messenger.

Many years later I learned why she believed the cardinal was a messenger from God. In her early eighties, she wrote two memoirs. Never intended for traditional publishing, they were gifts for the family, explaining her life as a young girl and mother. One chapter stood out for me.

In the height of the Great Depression, she was raising two young sons, my father and uncle, who were extremely sick with dangerously high fevers. She was afraid her sons would die. Young and very much alone, my grandmother began praying.

After a particular long night of walking the floors without sleep, she woke to the sound of a bird. Opening the front door, she found a perky red bird looking directly at her, singing his song from the porch railing. She wrote in her memoir, "I knew then my boys were going to be okay. I knew God heard my prayers and sent that little bird as a sign of hope."

My red bird came in May 2021. Early in the morning before the humidity and heat stripped the night air's coolness, he flew from the back porch to the fence post, where he sat perfectly still. I watched him closely, then, wanting a better view, I walked toward the fence post. He didn't care for that and flew to the pecan tree in the neighbor's yard, where he watched me and confidently sang his sweet song. It was then I began awaking from the fog of 2020, the fog of grief.

My brother died in early March 2021, following a horrific year with cancer diagnosed in the height of the COVID lockdown. My siblings and I gave him a church funeral at a little Baptist Church he had attended with his family. Located in the middle of nowhere Texas, the church was modest, but the preacher and his wife accommodated our needs, safely and lovingly. There were hand sanitizer bottles on every church pew.

Following the eulogy, the preacher asked us to share stories about our brother. All I could remember to say was how much I loved riding bikes with him when we were kids. We rode for hours, sometimes in the rain, but it always seemed to be in the summer, those forever summer days when we didn't go home until we knew it was time for supper. There were times we only had one bike, but it didn't stop my brother. He'd put me on the handlebars and off we went. My sisters remembered him singing and his funny stories. When it was time for my oldest brother to speak, he couldn't. He only shook his head, while tears rolled down his face.

Grief would not leave our family alone in 2020. It came one morning to Houston, when my pregnant daughter-in-law was alone. Grief came to my son, desperate for a plane in a faraway city, hoping to make it home to his wife. All the texts I sent, all the prayers I pleaded, could not stop the inevitable. The last text I received from my son read, "No heartbeat."

For months, my son called me, asking the same questions. And they always began with "Why?" I would listen, listen with such intensity I actually thought I would be given the right answer, the reason for such loss. It never came. I could never tell my son the reason why.

The suffering of 2020 was not only felt by my family, but by the entire collective, the family of men and woman around the world. I often thought we were united in a very tender way by the enormity of global suffering. We've begun to heal, just as the little red bird sang. God created a "world without end."

I've never stopped dreaming of little girls with sunburnt faces wearing glittery tee shirts at a church retreat in Palacios, Texas. Their sweet song, which they sang with every ounce of their being, forever serves as a reminder to me:

"All night, all day, angels watching over me, my Lord."

A Choir of Angels

Frederica Mathewes-Green

The two third-floor bedrooms in this old house are back-to-back, and the sisters sit in their back-to-back beds, staring up at the ceiling. The ceiling is very high overhead, perhaps fourteen feet, and trimmed with fancy white plasterwork. I'm about twelve, and my room, on the street front, is pale blue; my sister, age nine, has the next room back, pale yellow. We sit very still as we look upwards, listening intently, and don't know the other is doing the same. We both hear something going on in the attic, and we don't know what it is.

We moved into this big house, in the "old city" of Charleston, South Carolina, when I was about ten years old. My father loved his home town and did much of the early historic research. If you visit Charleston, as you walk around the old city, you'll notice wooden plaques on many houses detailing their histories; my father inaugurated that project, in the 1960s, and wrote many of the original descriptions.

He shopped wisely for a home, and we ended up moving into the highest house in the old city. It was called "O'Donnell's Folly," for the original owner, Patrick O'Donnell, took so long building and perfecting it that his fiancée married someone else. It is an immense and beautiful house (it has its own Wikipedia page), and the lovely arched doorway of 21 King appears in many photos online. (I was surprised when a friend told me this; I think of it as the doorway where I had my first kiss, a quick peck on the cheek.)

But the time I am talking about is some years earlier. We had recently moved from a normal-sized house to this one, and it was hard, settling in. We couldn't hear our mother calling us from the kitchen to get up for school; she had to use an intercom. The high ceilings, designed to shed heat, efficiently did the same in winter, when our bedrooms were desperately cold. Instead of two cozy bedrooms for three daughters, we were now in three vast rooms, twenty feet on a side, and felt the weight and presence of the house as something that could never mold itself to human life.

The old houses of Charleston often have a ghost or two. We heard sounds and saw things that were at sometimes merely odd, and at other times palpably dark. Usually only one of us would have the experience, and then share it with the rest. But with this presence in the attic, my sister and I both heard it.

It was the sound of voices singing. Yet it sounded unlike any music I was familiar with. It wasn't shaped like a song, with verse and chorus, rhythm and rhyme. Instead, the voices sang in very long lines of melody, as if singing paragraphs rather than poetry. They would join together and then separate, sometimes singing in unison, sometimes in chorus, with one voice holding a low note beneath the rest. There was no pattern I could figure out. First there might be a young man's voice, in a lengthy solo passage. A woman's voice, or a couple of voices, might join in with his. Sometimes they all sang together, and then it sounded like there were maybe five or six of them up there. The singers would take turns on the solo parts, and join together, and go back to solo again. It wasn't fancy—there was no instrumental accompaniment, no complicated harmony. Just long, long, fluid lines of song.

And it went on forever. "Don't they ever get tired?" I wondered. At some point I fell asleep.

In the morning I went up into the attic and looked around. I saw only the same retired furniture, empty picture frames, and boxes of outgrown clothing that were always there. There was nothing to *see*, which was frustrating, and I couldn't make the singers come back so I could question them. Looking around the attic was pointless. But from time to time my sister and I continued to hear them singing in the attic.

As I said, that wasn't the only strange occurrence in that old house. We saw and heard a number of things, most of them somewhat creepy. But this singing was different; it was comforting and gentle. And it somehow didn't sound like the singers were *performing*; they weren't singing the way people do when they're in front of an audience, projecting their voices mightily. Their singing sounded more like they were engaged in a serious, but enjoyable, project. It was how a group of friends might sound, if they gathered in a home to play some string quartets. The singers were serious about their work, and savored it at the same time, but they weren't doing it as if on stage. The motivation and goal was inside of them, and shared among them, and a mystery to the listeners in the rooms below. All the same, it comforted us; we could sense in it an innate goodness.

Eventually we stopped hearing that mysterious singing. Over the years I would sometimes think back to it, and wonder what it had been. It just wasn't like any kind of music I'd ever heard.

And then one day, some forty years later, I recognized that music again. I was in church for Vespers, and the same music was coming from the chanters' stand. It took the form of long lines of melody—known as chanting in the Orthodox Church—rather than verses of poetry. It was sung by one soloist, then a different soloist, then everyone together, in no predictable pattern. It was music that, to a little girl, would go on a long, long time. I had been hearing it at every service, ever since I became an Orthodox Christian, but I'd never recognized it till then.

When I heard that music in the attic, long ago, I sensed

that it was a good thing, unlike some of the other phenomena we encountered in that house. The singing brought with it a sense of blessing. It was angelic. And, now, I could sing along with the angels.

A Word to the Guy with the "God Bless" Sign by the Side of the Road

Angela Jackson-Brown

I try not to make eye contact
with you because if our eyes were
to meet, I might actually see inside
your soul. And the thought of being
that close to the essence of you scares
me, so each and every time I turn away
or I simply focus on the words you've
written on your sign.

Before, your sign said,
"Help! I'm homeless," and before that, "I'm hungry. Can you
spare some change?" Now, your sign simply says, "God Bless."
You ask for nothing—you simply shuffle around in some
bizarre dance, arms flapping like a strangled bird trying to
        get attention.
Any attention at all.

Each day you and your sign haunt me. I worry
that if I see your eyes, if I really look into them
I will find that you are no con man, no flim flam artist—
just a man who is down on his luck and has no greater

wish than to make me smile and send God's blessings
my way—and for that, you neither want nor desire for
me to pay.

The other reason I never meet your eyes is because I don't
want to see that you need more from me
than some nickels and dimes. I'm worried that
if I should happen to see your soul, I'll see a reflection of
the souls of my dad, my uncles, my brothers and my
         cousins who,
by fate's chance, never ended up on the side of the road
hoping God, some kind lady, or an angel
will offer them a look—a glance.

So, I don't look at you, because I don't have
time to be my brother's keeper. Not today. I've got schedules
to keep and deadlines to meet and for me to take on
your problems on top of my own
is way too much.

So, I look away. I look away.

Angels Passing Through My Life

Christa Allan

My most recent experiences with angels were unlike what I'd learned about them after attending twelve years of Catholic schools.

In the "Creation and the Angels" chapter from the *Baltimore Catechism*, we learned that angels didn't have bodies, some were good and some were bad, and we each had a guardian angel.

Granted, that was about as much information as kids in lower elementary could process. We seemed to accept the idea of their not having bodies, maybe watching Casper prepared us for that, but guardian angels? For each of us? My friend and I found it a wee bit creepy that these angels were with us ALL the time. The chapter didn't mention anything about girl and boy angels. Surely, God would appoint same sex angels for humans, right? Some of our classmates would save seats next to them in the cafeteria for their guardian angels, which Sister Robert had to call an end to because of table shortages.

For years, the guardian angel topic led to lively recess conversations. When you died, was your angel assigned to someone else? Like, how were there enough of them to be assigned to everyone in the whole world? Did they marry and make baby angels (of course we believed that babies arrived only after marriage)? But we still didn't know if angels were different sexes.

My Catholic mother had married my Greek Orthodox

father, and I worried he might not have his own guardian angel. Was he left out? What if one of us converted to Judaism? Would our angel be re-assigned? And if our guardian angels were with us always, did they talk to our parents' guardian angels and pass on information? Maybe we weren't supposed to know the answer to that question.

By sixth grade my fascination with guardian angels waned after Sister Michel slapped me in the face because she thought I'd stuck my tongue out at her. I hadn't. She happened to be standing behind my boy-crush Peter, and he'd stuck his tongue out at me first. But she couldn't see him do that, and no insisting, "He did it first," saved me. When my parents arrived for a conference, she denied the slap. But, the day after, she called me out of class and apologized. I remember wondering if my guardian angel had taken a nap or something. Surely, Peter's and Sister Michel's guardian angels could have interceded.

For the next eight years of high school and college, I had relegated the idea of having a guardian angel to the same box in my brain as to what I'd do in a nuclear attack—things I didn't have time to think about and/or had no control over.

Fast forward to the birth of my twin girls, babies number three and four in the lineup. That was the day I "abandoned" God because I felt He'd abandoned me. One of my daughters was born with Down Syndrome (DS), and I could not reconcile what I thought (then) was an undeserved tragedy. I was 29 years old when I became pregnant with the twins, below the statistical age of women bearing children with DS. We'd led a good life, attended church, were innocent of grievous behavior. If God could bring Lazarus back from the dead, why couldn't He have healed my child? Little did I knew that that her having DS would be the least of her problems: four major hospitalizations between the ages of eight and twelve months (one by Life Flight, one by ambulance), major surgery, and then a feeding tube for six months. Oh, and when they were a year old, I discovered I was pregnant.

What does all of that have to do with angels?

Almost forty years later, I think back about my life, and I realize that angels appeared for me when I needed them, and when I didn't know I did, and they started with Sarah. Not to say others hadn't appeared in my life, but I had no doubt that, starting with the girls' birth, God summoned His angels to minister to me. To us.

Before I left the hospital, someone had called a couple with a Down's child to come talk to us. I honestly don't remember who made the connection. But these strangers ministered to us in ways no one else could. Angels who prayed with us and reassured us and gave us hope. The small community in which we lived exploded with goodness. Angels who provided an almost never-ending procession of casseroles and desserts and company. Even a fund-raiser to help us with medical expenses. When it was time for Sarah to be hospitalized once again so doctors could decide if her gastro-tube could be removed, I was so emotional, so stressed that their answer might be, "No," I was terrified. A neighbor, whose family had taken in Sarah's twin (who didn't have DS), called me and volunteered to stay in the hospital with her. An angel whom, to this day, I thank God for, realizing what a gift she was to me.

Years later, I knew I was drinking too much, but it wasn't until someone we'd met months earlier confronted me that I agreed to admit myself for outpatient treatment. I never saw or heard from her again after we'd had breakfast that day; her family had moved while I was still in the hospital. Another angel sent by God to save not only my life, but my childrens' lives before I'd subjected them to my driving while I'd been drinking.

After Hurricane Katrina, we were ministered to by a host of people who helped us find jobs and a home.

When my first and only grandson died at thirty-one days, I was writing his eulogy when a butterfly landed on the page. I remember the sense of wonder I felt and knew that my guardian angel had sent me that moment of joy. And every day since, when a butterfly is near, so is Bailey.

And, just a month ago, my otherwise healthy forty-year-old daughter, who lives over eight hours away from me, had a severe stroke. From the moment I heard the news, I stormed the heavens with prayers asking God to send his angels to wrap themselves around her.

Piecing the chronology of events together, I have no doubt that God sent His angels every step of the way. My daughter's ex-husband (yes, they're still friends) stopped to see her; he had returned from offshore the previous day. When she didn't answer when he knocked on her back door, he thought the door might be locked. But her dog kept barking and running off; so thinking that was unusual, he tried the door knob. The door was open (unusual), and he was able to go inside her house.

Erin was on the sofa and, when she tried to stand, she collapsed. He took one look at her and called 911. The EMS could have taken her to a closer, smaller hospital, but they went straight to the Houston Medical Center. The doctors, after over two hours of surgery, removed a blood clot from the left side of her brain. The ER doctor told her sister that she probably wouldn't be alive had she arrived any later. Because of COVID, no one was allowed to be with her. She was released three days later, and with the exception of her ability to connect some of her dots, she is living alone again, driving, walking and talking without any signs of having had a stroke.

The miracle that she is today is due to a flurry of activity in heaven where angels propelled people to the exact places they needed to be to help her.

And going back to that *Baltimore Catechism* all those years ago, I found, " When God created the angels He bestowed on them great wisdom, power, and holiness," and "Our guardian angels help us by praying for us, by protecting us from harm, and by inspiring us to do good."

Sometimes God's gifts may not arrive in the packages we expect. Maybe no fluttering wings or unformed bodies or melodious voices, but people who listen to the still, soft voice inside them and appear in our lives to guide us, to protect us, and to love us.

And my gift? A guardian angel who's quite patient with a human-in-training.

Waiting For Her Angel

Renea Winchester

"Each morning when I open my eyes I ask God, 'Why am I still here?'" Mother confided.

It was not her way to take anyone into a confidence. In fact, I'm certain she wasn't truly speaking to me, but expressing exasperation to the spirit she called, "her angel." Mother, who suffered from agoraphobia—a relentless anxiety disorder—relied heavily on this angel to carry her through multiple treatments for many years. But as time wore on, Mother became frustrated with her body that had withered into a shell of what it once was; yet her mind remained laser-sharp. Her tone reflected her exasperation after years of struggling. As we say in the mountains, she and God were "on the outs." Meaning, she'd expressed her frustration with her Maker, yet He had done nothing to alleviate her suffering.

Each night as she went to bed, she readied her mind, and her heart, to leave this earth. Each night, she prayed to awaken in heaven. Yet when her eyes opened in the morning light, a blanket of darkness covered her.

She was still on earth.

Not in heaven with her mother, her father, her brother, and her baby sister who lived just long enough to draw a breath or two.

Mother was tired. She was ready, but at the same time, she wasn't. As with all who struggle with cancer, we hope—and pray—for a cure.

Mother had struggled for over a decade with ovarian cancer.

In the early years of her cancer journey, I made weekend trips from Atlanta back home to Bryson City, North Carolina while praying this diagnosis would bring us closer. I'd never been "enough" for Mother and she'd voiced her displeasure more times than I care to admit. We both wanted the same thing—a closer relationship—but as her health worsened, we couldn't find a way to become friends. It seemed we were always adversaries.

On this particular weekend, I drove to give Dad a break from Friday through Sunday. The visit also allowed me to spend time with Mother. As primary caregiver Dad had become just as homebound as Mother. And while metropolitan cities have people you can hire to run errands, prepare meals, wash clothes and mop the floors, rural areas do not offer those conveniences. Even hospice centers struggle for volunteers who can just sit with a patient in order to give caregivers a break. As with most visits, Sunday came quick. I kissed everyone goodbye and cried my way home. We'd said goodbye a thousand times, but during this visit she wanted to talk about her funeral. Instead of a traditional funeral with visitation, flowers, and a service, Mother wanted a wicker casket, which she called her "Baby Moses Casket." She was also clear on the services; there would be no visitation.

She'd seen an environmentally friendly casket in a magazine and ordered one without delay, having it delivered to the funeral home where it would wait until God called her home. "I don't want my last act as a human to have a negative impact," she'd explained with renewed excitement in her tired voice. "Bury me in my baby Moses casket. I'll be the first in Bryson City to have a one like it. Won't it be delightful?" She smiled. "I might even start a new trend."

At first, she wanted family members gathered around her

wicker casket, but as she sensed the end nearing, Mother opted for something private.

"Tell no one," she ordered as I wrote down her wishes in a notebook she kept at the ready. "When I die, don't you tell a soul. I don't want anyone talking about how good I look when I'm dead!"

I had nodded. "What about your nieces? They'll be devastated. Shouldn't they have the opportunity to say goodbye?"

"Already told me goodbye with that birthday party they threw me without asking," her voice tightened. Mother still hadn't recovered from their well-meaning party held two months prior. Her six nieces, whom she'd helped raise, traveled from out of state for one last party because one of the sisters had told the others, "This will be our last one with Catherine. Get yourself over to her house and tell her goodbye."

I had also been invited, but I declined.

Mother was never one for pomp, unless it was to celebrate others. I knew she wouldn't approve of this final hurrah.

After their impromptu gathering, Mother called me weeping uncontrollably.

She never cried.

"That was the cruelest thing they could have possibly done." Her breath came out as hiccups. "I am devastated. Why would they do this to me? Making people drive hours to see me. Where were they when I was well? Why did they wait until I was dying to tell me they cared about me?"

I hadn't the words to console her. Her feelings, and pain, were justified. She'd spent over a decade fighting ovarian cancer and what I call the social shunning of cancer. Where *had* they been when she needed them the most?

⁓

Early Monday, my cell phone rang. It was the hospice nurse. "Your mother is in the hospital. We'll hold her for you by pushing oxygen until you arrive," the nurse promised.

"No. Don't hold her for me," I begged. "Please, don't hold her. She's ready to go."

They held her.

Having worked in health care for many years, I know it is our human nature to hold fast, to linger so loved ones can say their final goodbyes, or experience closure in the case of prodigal children. But Mother and I had said our goodbyes. Each time we parted. We were both aware of the possibility the embrace could be our last.

I turned on the emergency flashers, pointed the car away from Atlanta, and returned to the rural mountains in record time.

⌒⸱⸱⸱∾

Ten years of surgeries, chemotherapy, radiation, hope for remission, and hair loss; hours of fighting to spend time with her family, of praying for one more day with her granddaughter, and (hopefully) praying for a better relationship with me, collapsed into one agonizing day inside a cramped hospital room.

I rushed to the visitor station where a helpful volunteer told me Mother's room number. I found my father standing outside the door. We didn't need to say anything. We knew Mother wasn't coming home today; she was going home to Jesus.

Inside, my hulk of a brother sat curled in on himself in the corner of the room. He gazed outside. He knew, but the wall he'd built was impenetrable.

Oxygen tubes whistled at the end of Mother's nose. The nurses fretted with the morphine drip and adjusted the bed up as high as possible so that mother sat upright, on her side, covered in warm blankets.

She was not conscious.

But, she knew who was in the room.

Remember, our loved ones *always* sense who is in the room. It doesn't matter that they cannot speak. They do hear us. They do feel our touch. They understand us. And it was with that knowing that I rushed to Mother, despite every bone in my body screaming otherwise. I pasted a smile on my face and forced a cheerful tone in my voice. Then I told the woman who birthed me, who raised me, and who loved me in her own way, a bold face lie.

"Mother, today is a great day to go see Jesus."

For her, it was a great day.

For me, it was agony.

For my father, the day ended almost fifty years of marriage.

For my baby brother, the moment burned forever-images of our mother's final breaths in his mind.

❧

The medical profession defines the sound patients make as they transition toward the end of life. They call it the "death rattle." When a person begins the transition, they cannot clear saliva from the back of their throat, cannot cough or swallow. As a result, a rattling sound erupts from the mouth. Sometimes it's a tiny wheeze; at other times it's a shrill scream-like roar.

The nurses turned Mother to ease the noise. Still, the sound persisted. I patted her shoulder, kissed her, and told her I loved her.

The rattle persisted. Sitting in the corner of the room, my brother flinched with each sound. "Think of it as snoring," I whispered in his ear. "Mama's just snoring. That's all. Don't let this moment be your last memory of her."

❧

The brain has a way of capturing last moments and replacing everything else with the most recent, the "last," moment. We may not remember childhood memories, but few can forget our loved one's final moments, for they remain with us until we draw our own final breaths.

I left my brother's side and returned to Mother, leaned over her bed, and told her another lie.

"It's ok to go."

Patients often *need* to hear these words from loved ones as a confirmation that we who remain will, *somehow*, navigate life without them.

"It's ok to go."

But it wasn't ok, not by a long shot. Not when all I *ever* wanted was to pile up in the bed with my mother and watch movies, to talk to her about books, to have her say, just once before God called her home, *I'm so proud of who you are.*

"Mama, it's ok to go. Your angel is waiting to take your hand."

Nurses and hospice volunteers often see this in their patients, the lingering. Patients who hold on until that prodigal child arrives. I like to think of the lingering as one last gift from God. But in Mother's case, my assurances didn't cause her to relinquish the hold on her earthly body. And so I stood at her bedside, saying again and again, "It's ok to go Mama. We'll make it. Go. Go see Jesus. He is waiting for you."

Hours crept by with only the snoring death rattle sounds and my reassurances filling the room. With each urging for Mother to let go, I began silently praying, "God, please . . . hurry. I'm not this strong."

Three o'clock arrived, the moment when my brother must leave and pick up his son from school. He spoke his goodbye to Mother and we exchanged a hug. "I'll be back in an hour," he said and held the door open for the nurse who entered to attend to Mother.

"Michael's gone to pick up the little one," I said while touching Mother's thin body. "It's ok to go."

Immediately, magnificent rays of sun filtered through the window shining directly on mother. My breath caught.

"Your angel is here to get you," I whispered to Mother. "Just reach out."

The rattle stilled.

The Truth About Angels

Jacqueline Allen Trimble

for MPT

If I have entertained angels unaware,
I hope I made pot roast. And served the good wine.
And used the good china. They deserve this
and much more given centuries of unpaid labor

and our dreadful behavior. Truth is
Raphael got it wrong. Do you think cherubs could do
what angels must dare, their little feet treading through
bordellos and battlefields? Their small hands holding

someone's son flat-lined in an alley or a kid with a kazoo
gunned down on his own street? The Bible is tight-lipped
on so many things, but I am sure Caravaggio
was also mistaken. There are no wings. Wouldn't fit

on buses, submarines, in the narrow doorways of hovels.
Way too conspicuous at lynchings and insurrections.
Also, they are not all hard, pale Renaissance bodies. I'm thinking,
raw-boned angels well-versed in grief and hunger. Corpulent

angels with arms and bellies large enough to cushion
the dying. Voices that sound more like buttermilk
pie or kindness than fire-breathing annunciators.
Can you see Botticelli's imagination float down

death row in the middle of the night? Angels
are meant to comfort, not traumatize. No togas,
shrouds, or some fluttery one-shouldered draping replete
with golden waist-cord either. Michelangelo

was worst of all. That weird ecstatic smolder
doesn't even make sense. Steely eyed, angels have seen
some things. Tried to make us do right. Suffered with us
as we have suffered, our wounded hearts plunging us and them

deeper into the depths. At what Dantean circle does an angel
abandon hope? Maybe Lucifer just couldn't take it anymore,
gave notice, then hurled himself off the ledge of Heaven.
Do you understand how little we know of love?

But God still sends them, these angels,
and they still go, doing what they can, even
as we pray one thing and do another. Over and over.
If they truly had halos, we would make them spin.

Rose's Angel

Mandy Haynes

This is a true story, although the names have been changed.

I worked as a pediatric cardiac sonographer for sixteen years at Monroe Carell Jr. Children's Hospital at Vanderbilt in Nashville, Tennessee. In that time I witnessed lots of angels and their mercies, but the story that comes to mind when I'm asked if I believe in angels isn't mine. It was told to me by a five-year-old girl and her adoptive father.

It all started when I went to the waiting room to call my patient back for her echocardiogram. I'd read her chart, so I knew that she was familiar with the process, but she was new to us. She had been born with a complex congenital heart defect called Tetralogy of Fallot, which is in fact four different heart defects. Ventricular septal defect—a hole between the right and left chambers of the heart, an overriding aorta, pulmonary stenosis, and right ventricular hypertrophy. My patient also had a large atrial septal defect, which had been repaired. Her name was Rose, and she and her family had recently moved to middle Tennessee. Today was the first time she would be seen at our clinic. I had no idea if she was a fighter, a crier, or if she liked having her echocardiogram. You never knew what you were going to get between the ages of one and six. Shoot up to eighteen years for that matter, so I liked to see what I was getting into.

I stepped into the waiting room and surveyed my prospects. There was only one girl close to her age, so that made it easy to figure out who I was about to call back. She was in a good mood, which made me happy. An adorable African American girl in a yellow dress sharing crayons and a coloring book with a boy close to her age. I assumed it was her brother who I would use to help me calm Rose down if I needed to. I made a mental note to get some crayons on my way back to the echo lab. I then looked to see what her parents were like. Sometimes the parents could be harder to handle than the patients. You had some who were high maintenance; they treated you like you were there to wait on them. Some had high anxiety and talked nonstop about how worried *they* were, which made it hard to focus on your patient. Some were just flat out rude and played on their phones or asked to turn the television to their favorite talk show instead of leaving it on the cartoon channel their child selected. Hard to believe but true. I always took a second to check everyone out before I called my patient's name. My coworkers used to tease me and say it was the writer in me and that I was looking for characters, but I liked to know what to expect.

There was a young guy with a Willie Nelson t-shirt, tattoos, and a baseball cap sitting across the room on his phone. Nope, he looked too young.

An older couple with a teenager sitting close by, a few other parents that I knew already, and a calm lady reading a book. Yes! I said almost high-fiving myself–that had to be her mother. They looked alike with their caramel complexions and calm, friendly dispositions. Whew, I thought, I'm in luck. The study was going to be hard enough to obtain the images of her complex defects and assess the site of her latest surgery. The mother looked like a pro.

"Rose," I called my patient's name and the little girl in the yellow dress jumped up from her seat so quick she knocked it over.

"Are you my doctor? Or are you my picture taker?" She pronounced picture as pitcher in a southern accent that surprised me.

I laughed and smiled at her mama. Good job, I thought, she's not afraid. I subliminally sent her mama a gold star.

"Yes, I am your picture taker. My name's Mandy," I told my patient and opened the door to take them back to the echo lab. But the lady didn't move.

"Come on, Daddy!" the patient ran across the room to the tattooed guy who was texting someone on his phone, "We've got to get my pictures."

I laughed and smiled at the lady I'd mistaken for her mother. She winked at me and grinned. I tried not to look disappointed as the guy spent a few more seconds on his phone. He hadn't even looked up from the screen. Then he took the little girl's hand, stood, and looked at me for the first time. I was taken aback at the look of worry on his face. It wasn't the look I'd expected.

"I'm sorry. My wife wants to be here to meet y'all. I was just seeing where she was. She had to go to work this morning, but she's on her way. She's stuck in dang traffic."

They might not have looked anything alike, but they sounded identical. And the way Rose held onto his hand and skipped up to me, I could see she felt safe and loved. I knew they had a story, but I had no idea how much I was going to love it.

Once we got back to the room where I performed echocardiograms and Rose was on the exam table, I told Rose's daddy that he could try his wife again. Mobile phones were usually discouraged in the lab because we wanted all the focus to be on the patient, but it was obvious that Rose wasn't afraid and that we were going to be just fine. She even asked if she could attach the stickers to her chest herself and asked if she could have cold gel instead of the bottle I took out of our warmer, because she explained, "That warm stuff feels like snot."

Rose told me about her scars and even showed me the

special spot to get pictures of her newest shunt. "Right here. Between these two ribs, not above it." She put her hand on mine and guided the transducer, and I'll be danged if she wasn't right. If she hadn't told me I would've spent a few minutes finding it. As I imaged her heart, she told me all about Tetralogy of Fallot and how her heart was made special.

I smiled at her daddy and told him Rose would make a great pediatric cardiologist.

"No lie. She knows more about her heart than we do," he grinned and reached out to pat her arm. I noticed his tattoo again, but before I had a chance to look closer, Rose asked me how her left ventricular function was doing.

"Do you like stories?" Rose asked after I answered her question.

"I love stories."

"Do you like angels?"

"Yes I do. I especially love stories about angels," I said.

"I knew it! Daddy! Tell her about my angel!"

Her daddy grinned and shook his head, "Let her work Doodlebug. She probably needs to concentrate and you ain't making it easy."

Rose and I both said, "Please tell the story!"

"Anyway, I'm almost finished thanks to Rose's help," I winked at her.

"Daddy," Rose crossed her ankles and put her hands behind her head, "Tell her the story—and start before y'all got the phone call."

This is the story her daddy, his name is David, told me.

Five years ago, David and Sharon were young newlyweds. They'd known before they were married that they wouldn't be able to have children, so they knew they wanted to adopt kids one day.

"Like in ten years or something. We hadn't been married long, but we've been sweethearts since elementary school, so we knew we'd do it, just not yet," David said, "We thought after we moved into a bigger house and spent some time, you know, just being married."

But a couple at their church had just become foster parents.

"They were older kids and needed a temporary home until their parents got some things figured out," David explained. "Me and Sharon thought we could do that. They were good kids who just needed a safe place to be for a while. We thought until we were ready to adopt a baby, it would be good to help some families. And it would be fun to have some older kids in the house–Sharon and me are both only children. We didn't have nieces or nephews.

"Next thing I know, we're taking classes to become foster parents," he laughed. "There are so many kids in the system it's awful. Sharon and I decided we'd start sooner than we'd originally thought–but we promised each other that we'd only bring home older kids who needed a place short term, and no kids with serious health problems. We weren't really set up for anything else."

"Well, just a couple of nights after we finished everything— all our classes and home inspections, and all that stuff you gotta do—we got a phone call. It was late and Sharon was asleep and I almost let it go to voicemail. I didn't recognize the number. You know, that by itself is kinda weird, because I don't answer calls I don't know. Anyway, I answered and it was a woman named Theresa Nevels. She said she was calling to tell us about a baby at our local hospital that needed help. I told her she had the wrong number. She said no sir, she had the right number and said both of our names," he reached out to squeeze Rose's knee and I got a good look at his tattoo.

It was an anatomically correct heart with three X's where Rose had had her three surgeries.

"The lady said, *You don't have to agree to anything now. The baby will not be leaving the hospital anytime soon. I'm just calling to see if you and Sharon would be willing to visit her in the hospital. She's all alone and the nurses would appreciate if someone could just be there for the baby.* Something like that, I don't even remember writing the information down, but the next morning I told Sharon about the phone call."

David checked his phone and smiled at Rose. "Your mama's parking the car. She'll be here in a minute."

"Daddy... don't stop telling the story."

"Sharon asked me who this Theresa Nevels was, and I didn't know—I'd assumed she was with social services or Child Services or whatever. I hadn't asked. We didn't even think about calling to verify anything—after breakfast we just went to the hospital. It was a Saturday, we were both home and we didn't have anything else to do. It's so weird when you look back at how everything just fell into place." David took off his cap and wiped his forehead. I noticed that he wiped his eyes too.

"At the nurse's station, we told them who we were and who we were there to see. I said that a Ms. Theresa Nevels had called us. Nobody questioned anything. We were given paper gowns and taken to a tiny room that had a funny looking baby bed with a top on it and this little, tiny baby in it. The nurse showed us where the hand soap and gloves were and said we could touch her hands and feet and pat her butt," Rose laughed, "and to talk to her as much as we wanted. Dang, she was so tiny, but she was tough. I put my finger by her hand to show Sharon how small it was, and Rose grabbed onto me and wouldn't let go. The next day, we went back to the hospital after church and got to hold her. We made arrangements to visit after work the next week. The nurses let us feed her and hold her as much as we wanted, and we both got good at burping her and changing diapers to give the nurses a break. But we kept telling each other that we weren't going to bring her home. It was one thing to do all that stuff there surrounded by nurses if we needed help, another thing to have her on our own."

"I had all kinds of wires and stuff stuck to me," Rose looked at me, "and I was scrawny."

"Sharon called the lady who we took the classes with, to

thank her for giving Ms. Nevels our number, and to let them know we were just visiting her—that we weren't prepared to take her. Well, she didn't know who Theresa Nevels was or anything about Rose. I thought maybe I'd misunderstood, and Theresa Nevels worked at the hospital. So I asked the lady at the nurses' station the next day. She had no idea who I was talking about. No information on a Theresa Nevels anywhere. She called her administrator, who had assumed we'd been sent by DCS, or the whatchamacallit. By that time, we'd gotten close to Rose and knew her schedule and the nurses all knew us. We'd decided that we weren't going to worry about it—we weren't ready to be foster parents anyway. Especially of a baby with such serious heart problems. So we just kept visiting her. But then it was time for her to leave the hospital and there wasn't anybody to take her. That's when DCS got involved and since we'd been cleared to be foster parents—and since we knew all about Rose—we just seemed like the right choice." David rubbed his neck and laughed, "About a year later we legally adopted her."

"Because my angel knew they were supposed to have me," Rose piped in.

There was a knock at the door and a young lady stuck her head in.

"Mama!" Rose yelled and sat up. "I'm done. I did good!"

"You must be Sharon," I caught Rose as she hopped off the table. "It's so nice to meet you. I've heard a lot about you."

"Rose, I hope you didn't talk her ears off," Sharon said as she tried to help Rose put her shirt on. "She loves to talk."

Sharon mouthed the words, *how'd it look?* and I gave her a thumbs up.

"Yeah she does," her daddy said, and they both grinned at each other. Sharon gave up trying to help Rose who wanted to put her shirt on all by herself and walked over to David. She gave him a kiss on the cheek and wiped his eyes.

"So, did you ever find out who Theresa Nevels was?" I asked.

"No, never," David said.

"Oh, that's what y'all were talking about." She smiled, shrugged her shoulders, and turned to me, "Nobody knew who she was or anything about her."

"I know her," Rose pulled her shirt over her head and smiled. "She's my angel."

All in the Family:

Mothers, Fathers, Sisters, and Grandfathers

A religious person may find the supernatural they seek in
the story of my grandfather's death. An atheist might see a
sweet older widower, heavily medicated, talking in his sleep.

—Wendy Reed,
"The Day of the Dead"

Death is merely a bridge that we must cross over,
and although it feels like we are separated from those we love
we aren't, not really, because pieces of those we love will
always dwell inside of us. Parts of them leave, but the parts
that matter, their
undying love, remain as long as we have memory and breath.

—Angela Jackson-Brown,
"When A Mother Leaves Her Child"

The Day of the Dead

Wendy Reed

"Day of the Dead": "the idea of having a city-wide parade
of people wearing hallowe'en-like costumes started only
in 2016, the year after Metro-Goldwyn-Mayer invented a
Day of the Dead parade in Mexico City for the James Bond
film Spectre."—Wikipedia

When Granddaddy died, I was making a documentary about
apprentice morticians. I'd obtained legal permission from the
funeral director program at the local community college; signed
on interesting-sounding and willing students—Jackie Brown and
Jody Foster; scheduled remotes in Colma, California, the City
of the Dead (a necropolis with one thousand times more dead
than living) and in Las Vegas, City of Conventions, including
the Expo for the International Association of Funeral Directors.
I'd also rewritten yet again my script outline, which included the
process, beginning in the classroom and ending with a funeral. I'd
even secured local funeral homes as locations for shoots.

But one dilemma remained: I needed a body.

Until you've approached complete strangers—grief-stricken
and in casket-choice limbo—and asked to use their deceased
loved one in a film, you have not seen incredulous. I explained to
them that I only needed a few close ups. That the face wouldn't

be seen. No identifying marks would show. They mostly stared. I tried begging. I tried bribing. I even offered to let them be in the show. They found words: "Are you out of you mind?"

The hospital that admitted Granddaddy was on the same side of town as the funeral program, so I stopped by to visit him. He was 93, but until the day before had lived independently, even providing care for my grandmother—Bigmama to us fifteen grandchildren—as her health deteriorated. Someone probably should've taken away his driver's license but the main place he drove—the grocery store—was only a few blocks away. As Bigmama's faculties declined, an obsession with paper towels emerged, which necessitated emergency trips to the store if she ran out. The closest Granddaddy ever came to complaining was when he told my aunt, "I could've bought a paper mill by now." It couldn't have been easy, yet not once over those years did his smile fade. He spent free time in the back yard "piddling"—picking up pecans or moving stuff in and out of his storage house. He couldn't throw anything away, a trait I'd associated with living through the Depression but has been recently popularized as hoarding. Hospice eventually came to help with Bigmama. Mother, the oldest of the kids, lived next door and popped in and out, and the rest pitched in as they could, but Granddaddy was there with Bigmama every day and night until the end.

"Well, look at you!" I said, not surprised that Granddaddy looked so healthy. He *was* healthy. His eyes lit up the whole hospital room as he smiled. In the corner chair, Uncle Gene sat sentry, looking every inch the Army Depot Guard he'd been. I'd never once seen him without my aunt.

"She stayed home with a migraine," he said.

After kissing Granddaddy's forehead and letting him pat

my arm, I carefully climbed onto the bed by his feet. I can't remember what we said but I remember the way he lit up again when the nurse came in. She stopped to let him pat her, too, then tended to his IV. Maybe he said she was his favorite nurse or maybe she said he was her favorite patient. Maybe he called her a beautiful angel or she told him he was the sweetest man, I'm not sure, but for some reason, his glow seemed to increase a few watts. She finished but he wasn't ready for her to leave, so she stayed and flattered him a little longer.

It's been said that laughter is the best medicine and touch has the power to heal, but I'd wager that flirting with the nurse was good for Granddaddy's soul.

For as long as I can remember Granddaddy was a patter. Whether he'd just met you or had known you forever, he'd reach for your arm and the percussion would begin, maybe stopping after a couple of beats or continuing on as if translating *War and Peace* into morse code. My children's father Scott said that he'd never met anyone like Grandaddy. On our first date, as we walked to the car, Grandaddy called, "Nice looking automobile" from his driveway next door and ambled over for an introduction. Scott's car was a shiny Celica Supra but I suspect since my parents were at work, it wasn't the car Grandaddy wanted to check out. I imagine it was his granddaughter's date. He took Scott's hand as if to shake it, but the patting began. This must've been confusing to Scott—his own grandfather was a retired cop—Vice squad—so Scott knew the importance of first impressions. At some point Grandaddy leaned in. Maybe Scott thought Grandaddy was going to instruct him what time to have me home but that's not what happened. Scott turned toward him and he felt lips. Not on his cheek, like an Italian greeting. No. On his *LIPS*.

They were there. Then they weren't. It was over.

Our date was the school play, so I told Granddaddy we

didn't need to be late and said bye. Seems like we rode awhile before Scott spoke.

"Your grandfather kissed me on the lips."

I nodded.

"He's Irish," I said, as if that explained everything.

Granddaddy's siblings had also been touchers. With names like Pete, Doshie, and Flossie, they sounded more like a fluffle of bunnies than a family of great-aunts and uncles. They even sneaked off together, but instead of Mr. McGregor's garden their forbidden destination was a taffy pull. Apparently taffy gets quite hot. Aunt Doshie didn't wait long enough for it to cool and badly burned both of her hands.

"I won't be able to do the milking tomorrow," she said, afraid this would tip off their parents. Granddaddy hatched a plan. "I'll go and do the milking for you," he said. "You wear gloves until the blisters pop."

But once home, the blisters were too painful to hide. The fluffle got busted. Granddaddy always maintained that the "whoopin" he got was worth it because he met Bigmama there. Not only did he get the girl, it was the beginning of the story of a marriage that lasted for seventy-seven years. As for Aunt Doshie's story, she'd just laugh even though she got burned on both ends.

Granddaddy's voice was a little weak, so I was doing most of the talking. When the phone rang my uncle answered. I could tell it was my aunt, the fourth and middle of Bigmama and Granddaddy's seven kids. I mentally went down the list of my cousins, trying not to leave anyone out. I counted fifteen. I was the seventh. Also smack in the middle. Granddaddy dozed off and Uncle Gene hung up the phone. It dawned on me that we three had never before been in a room together by ourselves.

Our family usually visited in numbers. Sometimes we might gather in a small pack but typically we preferred the whole herd. Our hospital trio didn't even constitute a small pack. By definition, Grandaddy was the patriarch, but fluffles do not produce alpha males. Me, the middle grandchild, and Gene, not even blood but an in-law married to the middle child, constituted the most unexceptional members. We were the most middling of the middle, the least, you might say, of these. The higher-ranking members—including my mother and the two males, who may have jockeyed every so often for alpha position—were absent for good reason.

Long months of cooking, cleaning, washing, dressing, calculating medicine, coaxing Bigmama in after calls from the neighbor that she was taking the garbage out again, naked, and unceasing purchase of paper towels had taken a toll. Though neither a surprise nor unwelcome, the finality of Bigmama's death—its complete irreversibility and the surreal vacuum left when someone, who has always been there, no longer is—landed like a physical blow. They'd been preparing for her death of course. Grief, though, can't be rehearsed. It can't be practiced. It only arrives when it's too late.

Bigmama had only been gone fifteen days.

"Funerals," according to the funeral program director, "are not for the dead. They're for the living because they offer closure. Saying goodbye helps people start to grieve." He advocated for open caskets.

The director had heard of the Lazarus effect—where a clinically dead person comes back to life—but never experienced it. Two of the thirty-eight cases that have been documented reached the morgue, and one case had to be unzipped from the body bag. The eeriest thing the program director had ever experienced, however, was occasional body noise—trapped gases being expelled.

During Bigmama's last days, their house hummed like a bee-hive, adults and children coming and going, songs and prayers buzzing around. No one knew when they left if they'd said their last goodbye. As she was rolled from side to side and diapers put on and off, red marks and purple bruises bloomed everywhere like strange flowers. She'd been apple-shaped—like mother—thick around the middle but thin everywhere else. Now there wasn't anything thick about her. Without the underlying cush-ion, her skin hung in certain places like drapes. In other places, like the backs of her hands, her skin was paper-y thin, almost translucent. If I looked long enough I might see down to the bone. If I rubbed too hard, it would tear.

Mother and my aunts needed to get some sleep, so I took a night on the couch by Bigmama's bed. As I dimmed the lights and adjusted her pillow, I was vaguely aware that something inside—somewhere deeper than our deepest secrets and in the oldest part of our brain, within the core of our squishy cauliflower, if you will, where the hippocampus and friends play at making meaning—my foundation was shifting. I had accepted as a child that the praying sounds Bigmama sometimes made came from the Holy Ghost be-cause it was what I was told, and also probably because the sounds were so spooky. I'd also been taught that the body was the temple of the Holy Spirit by my Sunday School teacher, who lived next door on the other side. She'd mentioned to our class that even better than being saved by Jesus was being sanctified by the Holy Ghost, I marched immediately down to the altar and placed my order, where it was explained to me that it didn't quite work that way.

"Usually it's a process," I was told, and something about anointing followed. I was confused because it had sounded so simple. "Maybe you should wait for it to happen. Give it some time." But I didn't want to wait for delivery. Tomorrow wasn't guaranteed. I could be raptured any moment. I was, after all, already eight. The clock was ticking.

In retrospect, I blame McDonald's. Only a few blocks from my house and a block and a half away from my church, the restaurant pioneer had set down a pair of its Golden Arches. Beneath them, impatience was rewarded. Food was fast and came with a choice, dine in or drive thru.

As I stood beside Bigmama in the shadowy light, more than a quarter-century had passed since I placed that sanctification order. Along with producing the mortuary-student documentary, I was co-editing a book *All Out of Faith*, which dared suggest that "spiritual" and "religious" were not synonyms. It criticized dogmas and One Size Fits All. Bigmama literally believed the Holy Spirit dwelled within her. Standing beside her, I didn't want to feel like a critic. I wanted to feel like a granddaughter. I closed my eyes and took a deep breath. I couldn't help notice how the supposed dwelling of the holy temple smelled. I opened my eyes. Some temple. I took a step back. What *had* the Holy Spirit been thinking? I took another step back to get a good breath. What kind of design was this anyway?

As an adult, what I had learned of the body, of life, of life's beginnings, and its natural end, death, collided with beliefs that my grandparents held dear. Church hadn't only shaped their beliefs, it was the cornerstone of their belief system. Many of their beliefs were simply untrue—dreaming about death doesn't mean someone will have a baby, prayer doesn't lower scarlet fever, and the delicious feeling they got at Ole' time singings and prayer meetings happens in many experiences that aren't religious, including meditation and marching. It comes from the synchronization of respiration and heartbeat.

Born at the turn of the century, they'd witnessed mind boggling progress—space travel, computers, TV with too many channels to count, and antibiotics that would've saved their first born's life. Such advances were taken in stride by my grandparents. *There was no telling what they'd come up with next.* They were not ones to get bogged down in the details, the behind the scenes workings or methods that drove such progress. But for over ninety years their system had worked. I don't think either graduated school and they married as teenagers: Bigmama at fifteen, Grandaddy at eighteen. I didn't want to jeopardize anyone's stability by questioning the construction that made them feel safe.

Cracks, though, had been forming in my childhood foundation for some time. Although terrifying, eventually it became too uncomfortable to stay in a structure that felt limited, constraining, possibly dangerous. As I stood before my grandmother's familiar, if smelly, holy temple I knew I would need a different architect.

I'd only been gone from their house for about ten or fifteen minutes when my cell phone rang. I turned the car around immediately. Everyone had heard about my documentary, I think. I might've even mentioned my dilemma. But the day Bigmama died, no one brought it up. Those days are a bit of a blur, I confess, but what I can tell you is this: the only thing worse than asking strangers to use their loved one's body is asking your kin.

Suffice it to say Bigmama does not appear in the documentary.

Granddaddy didn't seem as lost without Bigmama as I imagined he would. Seventy-seven years of marriage to someone is almost unfathomable. The "kids" took care of the details and may have had a different take on how he coped in the wake of her death but I do know that Granddaddy's hospitalization came as a surprise to all of us.

"Pneumonia," the doctor diagnosed.

"How on earth!" we said.

I never discussed The Big Bang or Creation or the evolution of life—bacteria or humans—with my grandparents or asked if they'd ever examined their beliefs. But In our post-truth and ideologically polarized world, where conservatism and religion are often pitted against science, and demagogues use mis- and dis-information to prey on the vulnerable, it seems belief is worth a closer look.

The 2018 *Psychology Today* article "What Actually Is a Belief? And Why Is It So Hard to Change?" illustrates the rigidity of beliefs and the lengths we will go to rationalize and protect them. Numerous journals note that belief systems may be both necessary and inaccurate, with book after book illustrating how the brain, an energy-conserving organ, evolved tools and short-cuts not to increase accuracy but to save energy. Patternicity, the tendency to see false connection in unrelated or meaningless data, and pareidolia, the tendency to recognize patterns or objects in things such as a face in a cloud, allow us to process vast amounts of information and quickly categorize, evaluate, and jump to conclusions. The bottom line for the brain is to live another day. Time spent analyzing rustling leaves might mean we became lunch. Better to run and enjoy tomorrow than focus on the facts. Evolutionarily speaking, the brain is prone to error. It's an adaptation that works.

While antibiotics were snaking their way through plastic tubing into Granddaddy's arm and work stress was pulling at me from different directions, in the corner my uncle remained on guard. Three is a symbolic number, the first true number according to Pythagoras. It's the number of times a Muslim husband must say I divorce thee to make it legal. It's triangular. Geometric. It's fantastic. It's little pigs and wishes and billy goats gruff. Three can also be one too many.

I didn't want to tire out Granddaddy, who had been dozing in and out and finally seemed to be sleeping soundly, so I decided it was time to go. That's when it happened: Grandaddy sat up. His eyes were still closed, and his right arm rose slowly in the air. With his arm aimed toward the sky as if reaching, he mumbled something, and then fell back on his pillow.

My uncle and I looked at each other. I raised my eyebrows: What in the world was that?

According to my memory, my uncle and I joked that Bigmama hadn't liked Granddaddy flirting with the nurses and reached down to yank him up. If he wasn't careful she might succeed next time.

But memory is part desire. It's one of the brain's conservation tools and is far less reliable than we tell ourselves. I dialed my Aunt and Uncle to fact-check my recollection.

"I don't remember you saying that," he said. "He did kinda sit up and lift his arm, though."

He thought the strange part happened when my Uncle Buddy had taken Granddaddy to visit Bigmama's grave the day before Granddaddy got sick and reported, "He wasn't sick or nothing." But as they turned to leave, Granddaddy waved to the grave and said, "I'll see you in a couple of days, Baby."

I'd forgotten that part. But my Uncle forgot I'd even been at the hospital.

The brain is also a story addict. With the help of all the energy-saving devices, a story is born. Story bears meaning. It makes and re-makes memories. It reinforces and entrenches belief. In cahoots with the ventromedial prefrontal cortex we write the story of our Self. Story evolves with our brain but it still serves at the brain's pleasure. Long after the brain's circuitry ceases, however, story has the power to live on.

The day after the cemetery visit, Granddaddy fell ill and was hospitalized. The day after that, not long after sitting up in bed and reaching toward the heavens, he died. It was November 2, 2002.

Not once did I think about him being in my documentary.

Writing this essay has been difficult because the last thing I would ever do is break my grandparents' hearts, and I don't know how they would feel about my lack of religiosity. I'm sure they wouldn't have dreamed of examining their beliefs. Or care that MRIs and optogenetics allow us to see the brain at work and better understand how we evolved. Hearing that we're still guided by the primitive core of our brain much more so than free will, despite what we tell ourselves, would likely just be evidence to them of our original sinful nature. What we see and interpret is always based on what we are primed to see. *That*—no matter how rational we try to be—is a fact. A religious person may find the supernatural they seek in the story of my grandfather's death. An atheist might see a sweet older widower, heavily medicated, talking in his sleep. I could include additional facts: Granddaddy visited the cemetery on October 31, and Dia de los Muertos is commemorated on November 1-2. I could also ask: What does it mean to die on the Day of the Dead?

Fact: My grandparents passed down their love of story to me.

Memory: The way they fed me cornbread sitting in their kitchen when I got a catfish bone stuck in my throat.

Truth: The best stories break our hearts open.

Meaning: I was lucky to be their granddaughter and know they loved me, no matter what.

The End

Lisa Gornick

When my father became terminally ill at the age of eighty-five, something remarkable happened: I discovered a depth of devotion to him I'd not known was there. This came as a surprise because of what I had long thought was the nature of our relationship—warm and for the most part free of conflict, but marked by a distance between us, a distance, in part, due to our each being fiercely independent. We'd both moved out of the family home shortly after I turned seventeen, and hadn't spent more than a dozen nights under the same roof since. Once, when he was in his early eighties, about to embark on one of his far-flung journeys, and I'd suggested he carry a cellphone, he replied that the point of traveling was to be out of touch. Even when he was home, weeks would sometimes pass without our speaking—and then, impromptu, he'd come for Sunday dinner: pour himself a scotch from the bottle we kept for him, and inevitably the atlas or globe would find its way to the kitchen table while he discussed Russia's role in World War II with my younger son, or Lucretius' prescient understanding of atomic theory with my older son, or developments in plastics and LED technology with my husband. My own pursuits, as a psychoanalyst and then as a fiction writer, were a language as a scientist he didn't speak—Freud, in his view, a witch doctor; his interest in contemporary fiction having halted with Philip Roth—though he did ask me each time I served him my roasted cauliflower how I cooked it.

With his illness, everything changed. We had a shared project: unearthing a diagnosis, and then attempting to synthesize three radically different treatment recommendations from six stellar medical centers. I hadn't talked to my father daily since I was a child, but now we were in touch every day. Rather than feeling like a burden, the conversations filled me with admiration for my father's dispassionate view of his situation and his lack of self-pity. He'd been well most of his life and now he was not. He did not believe he had been dealt a bad hand; rather, this was a hand. He wanted to live for as long as he could maintain a decent quality of life—but he never sugarcoated the grim prognosis. Most of all, he remained himself: living alone, reading *The New York Times* and *The New York Review of Books*, setting himself mathematical problems, going to movies and lectures, cooking ribs in his toaster oven.

As the months passed and my father grew weaker, as much from the treatment as from the progression of his illness, he became essentially homebound. Because he insisted that he needed no more help than the same cleaning person he'd had for years, three hours every other week, I began to visit him most days. He refused to lock his front door, so I would let myself in, and if he was napping, as he often was, I would stealthily wash the piled-up dishes and bag the trash. Puttering about, surrounded by the relics from his life—the samovar his grandparents had brought from Russia, the fossils from Montana, the yellow pads with his calculations—I would wonder about the dedication to him I'd discovered, aware that it came from somewhere primal, from something that must have transpired between us when I was very young.

A year after my father commenced his journey into illness, he collapsed in the middle of the night. In the emergency room, it was my father, not the medical staff, who correctly identified the reason for his collapse—and it was he who discerned that he'd fallen off a cliff and was now plummeting, not drifting, toward death. Had he been able to control his fate, he would have ended his life then, rather than returning home bedridden. His affairs were in order and he felt, he told me, at peace. But I was not: There were things I still wanted to talk with him about.

But what? What did I want to say to him?

What I wanted to tell him, I realized, had to do with the deep influence, I'd come to see, he'd had on my pursuits, an influence that had been obscured by our glaring differences and the divergent paths we'd taken. By now, though, he was sleeping nearly all the time and when he was up, it was rarely for more than twenty minutes at a stretch.

I planted myself next to the hospital bed we'd set up in his living room. When his eyes opened, I said, "Dad, could we talk?"

With a look of curiosity on his face—this was something new—he said, "Okay."

"There are some things I'd like to tell you." I took his hand. "I know I've never said anything like this before, but I want to tell you what I'm grateful to you for."

I told him how to my surprise—surprise because family lore was that he was an absent-minded professor, his mind more on the equations that describe wave formations than on the inner lives of humans—I'd come to see how perceptive and tolerant of me he'd always been.

"Do you remember when I was in second grade and I was terrified of an icy hill outside my school?"

He gave me a half-smile.

"All that winter you would park the car and, taking my arm, walk me to the door. You never made me feel badly that I was afraid of slipping."

"And later that year, when I was scared of a dead bird on the sidewalk, you never chided me for taking a different street so I would avoid seeing it. You just accepted that about me."

My eyes welled with tears as I reminded my father that after my younger son was born and we were all lost in the bliss of a new baby, he was the one who privately warned me not to overlook the dislocation for our older son, no longer the solitary prince. How, more recently, when there'd been some family discord about which I'd remained silent, he urged me to talk with him about it—and then, never taking sides, distilled what I said in a way that left me feeling utterly understood. Only now could I see that what I'd learned from his way of absorbing distress without minimizing it or compulsively giving advice were at the heart of my work as an analyst and novelist.

When I finished, he said, "Thank you, dear. I'm grateful for your having told me. But now I need to close my eyes."

He closed his eyes and slept and I sat by his bed, and when he woke up, I gave him some apple juice and said, "Dad, there's something more I want to tell you."

He nodded, and I could see that this conversation was important to him too. And here's the second thing I told him. I told him that I understood now that I'd become a writer because of him. That behind my own drive to tell stories was what I'd learned and been inspired by and imprinted with from his omnivorous curiosity and adventurous spirit—a spirit that led him to the wild places in Central Park, where there are feral raccoons and waterfalls, and to corner bars in Tehran and Baku, where he'd listened to the tales of men who work in concrete factories and on oil rigs. He'd made me believe that with bravery and persistence and creativity, narratives could be fashioned about the genesis of the universe, the scaffolding of scientific discoveries one atop another, the folding and unfolding of ethnic identities within the shifting borders of nations.

"Well, I'm glad," he said.

During my father's final week, I watched his death arrive, footstep by footstep—the end of foods and then liquids and finally consciousness itself—with a crescendo that reminded me of childbirth. "I am not afraid," my father had told me, and I realized that I, too, was unafraid: that he'd shown me, a child who had once taken circuitous routes to avoid a bird corpse, how simple and natural death can be.

Sitting at his bedside his last afternoon, I saw that he'd reached the portal: his eyes open, his gaze fixed on the ceiling, his breath ragged. I swabbed his parched mouth and cracked lips, and put faith in our hospice nurse's claim that he could still hear us.

"Dad," I said, "it's very near, you are almost there. I hope you remember what I told you," and then I said again how very much I loved him and would miss him.

The final thing I learned from my father is something I never got to tell him. As I stayed with him through the evening after he died, holding his hand, feeling his body cool, I was no longer surprised by the depth of my dedication to him. I understood whereby it came, and I was thankful to have discovered it: this devotion that had supplanted obligation and guilt and carried me through my father's final year, down a river of filial love as ancient, I imagine, as humanity itself.

Letters to Little Rock

Jennifer Horne

These five poems are from a series I am writing about my father, Allan W. "Dick" Horne, who died of pneumonia January 21, 2018. Born in a small town in Arkansas in the midst of the Depression, he was the eighth and youngest child in his family and the only one to graduate from high school. His brothers and sisters gave him the nickname "Dick," perhaps influenced by the popular Horatio Alger story of a boy called "Ragged Dick" who works hard and rises out of poverty. Indeed, from a childhood in which my father helped his family survive by picking peaches or doing other farm work, then later having a paper route, he became determined to do more in life. He joined the Navy and served in the Korean War on an aircraft carrier. When he came home, he went to college and then law school on the G.I. Bill, working in private practice as an attorney and also enacting reforms as state insurance commissioner. He started his first job as a lawyer three days after I was born, in Little Rock, Arkansas, in 1960, and he worked until three weeks before his death, at age 85. These poems, all second-person addresses, have become a way of continuing the conversation with him beyond his death, and also of telling the story of his life and the stories he told about it. My working title for the collection is "Letters to Little Rock."

Tears

On your last visit,
you left your tears behind.

Four little plastic tubes,
ampoules, you'd call them—

the word sounding old-fashioned,
like the way you signed

your full name
on the card reader,

taking your time
to get it right

though it would quickly disappear,
there, and then not there.

Lines

In North Carolina, my neighbors
had a red phone booth in their yard
amongst the camellias,
rhododendron, hellebores.
The British kind, enclosed
like a many-windowed room,
with TELEPHONE at the top, the kind
I used to stand in every Sunday
when I called from my year abroad in Oxford
and sometimes cried with homesickness.

When you were dying in Arkansas
and I was off teaching in Carolina,
it was snowing hard, and dark,
and I couldn't get to the phone booth.
I'd found an old phone in a closet.
I picked up the heavy receiver,
put my finger in a numbered circle
and dialed, 664-3608, thinking if you
were anywhere reachable, it would be
at the number I'd memorized at age 6,
going off to first grade.

I told you what a good father you'd been,
wished you peace and freedom from pain.
I told you it was OK to go, the way you told me
I could spend a year away from home
in a country you'd never seen
among people you'd never met
because you trusted I would find my way,
because you knew I needed to go,
because although you didn't like yard work
you were a natural gardener, always
encouraging me in the direction of growth.

What lines still connect us—
invisible and taut—beyond
the red box, the squat black phone,
the slim silver magic you learned?
Without a grave to visit, I walked
in the local cemetery, spoke
to any stone that spoke to me.
Once—I swear it—I found
golf clubs on a grave, and thought
to speak of it next time you called.

Playing Hooky

I thought you were gone. But, remembering the story you told of getting mad at your fourth-grade teacher who punished you for erasing your math problem when you knew she'd said it was okay, I wonder if you're just skipping, the way you skipped the rest of fourth grade, waiting until your mother left to take the bus to her job at the ladies' clothing store, watching her from the strip of park on the avenue and then returning home. It was the injustice you felt so keenly, like having to wear the stupid mask when your lungs couldn't do the job on their own. Maybe, I tell myself, you're just playing hooky now, skipping life for a little while, outside somewhere, not in a park but on the golf course, free to walk the cart-paths, dream of your third hole-in-one.

Call me from the airport gate, waiting for your plane home, with your well-worn briefcase and zippered carry-on hanging bag. Call me from the high room of a conference hotel, your voice filled with wonder at the beautiful view. Call me from your office looking over the Arkansas River, the little boy from the Ozarks, the grown man with stacks of case files in a pattern only you understand and a sign next to the disposable coffee cups you plan to reuse:

"Do Not
Touch or Remove
Any Cups In
This Office
Thank You—Allan W. Horne."

The Messages

In Ireland, what I call "running errands"

they call "getting the messages."
Along with the ordinary comes the coincidental,
along with the daily, the convivial.
Along with the necessary
may come the serendipitous,
chores not incompatible with connections.
Taking a necessary walk
around the pretty campus
with my alert brown dog,
I watch her sniff socially at a blade of grass,
reading, getting her messages,
stopping stock still to stare at things I can't perceive.

I think maybe I'm willing to believe—
or at least not willing to not believe—that
you might be getting a few messages through.
The week before you died,
calling from the hospital,
you told me we'd see each other soon,
we'd *find a way to get together,*
one way or another.
It's not like you to knock or tap
or blink the lights
or shimmer. But sometimes, not looking,
I still catch the odd, peripheral glimmer.

A Thing or Two

I got your message, the one
where you said you had some things
to tell me but there were one
or two barriers in the way, or layers, things
you couldn't quite get through. It's one
time-tested mode to speak through dreams, another thing

entirely to tell me but not tell me. Can anyone
know where the messages come from? A thing
like this, an instance, might lead one
to wonder about the liminal nature of things.
You were smiling but perplexed, like that one
time you tried to learn the computer, a thing
I use now to skip place and time like a stone.
Now I'm thinking, what if your message was just the thing
you told me, and not one blessed thing more?

Poems For My Sister Jennifer

Ann Fisher-Wirth

These poems are about my sister Jennifer, who died on October 1, 2019, having been sick for five months with cancer.

Komm süßer Tod

Come sweet death, my sister wrote in her secret notebook
at thirteen, shortly after our father died. *Come,
sweet death, for I grow weary of my living.*

*I am a tumbling stream
that burbles over rocks and swerves around boulders,
but at last falls silent when it spreads to meet the ocean.*

Snooping, I read what she wrote.
I had no words for how he lingered, then collapsed,
how his brown and pink plaid laprobe
held the smell of his decay—

Now evil seeds keep scattering through her body.
I keep wanting to tell our mother, long since dead,
She's sick, she needs you, go to her quickly.

White Wave

And now the water glistens on the sand.
It's all drawn back, your life,
vanishing like the wave,

our mother named you Jennifer—
white wave—
so, slip gently, evening is coming.

Every time... every time...
you said to me, holding me in infinity
with your eyes as I was leaving.

You could barely speak,
but such peace there was between us.
One time will be the last time...

Inhabitation

A year ago midsummer, we visited Magnolia Grove,
you with your newly shaved head, and when
I introduced you, Sister Boi and Sister Peace,
likewise bald, embraced you.
        Heat gathers,
every day hotter than the day before.
Something lives in our walls again,
scrabbling behind the bricked-up fireplace,
and ants spill out from infinitesimal cracks
in the corners. Apricots rot before they're ripe.
My days in near seclusion

creep through the hours and surrender to sleep.
Or to twitches, as if I'm a rag doll shaken.

.

I can't tell you how I miss you.
I keep wanting to phone you,
ask something you would know,
with your elephantine memory—
what year our father went to Korea,
when and how our grandparents died.
To ask if you remember all that past—
But one night, as I lay there twitching,
trying to sleep, you came
through the shining membrane
between life and death, so that I saw you,
and was you, gaunt edifice, cage of bone,
and the clear, diminishing flame
that was still, in that second, my sister.

And Behind Us, Only Air

Ten days from death, she glows, sitting beside me
on their deck, scarf wrapped around her head.

She's leaning toward me. I have a cold
so I'm leaning away, afraid to give her

one more thing to fight, and it hurts
that someone seeing this photograph

might think I'm avoiding her. She's softly
smiling at the photographer—her husband—

on this my last visit to see her. I feel messy,
unfinished; there's too much of me,

I'm too given over to life, and all that has
been stripped from her. She has gone

beyond grief. Not yet, though, is she skeletal, quite.
Just luminous.

Persimmons

My sister said, *I would like to write
about these persimmons but I can't.*

Along the street they hung,
glossy and taut among the leaves,

all of light in their red-orange flesh,
like breasts, like buttocks or wombs

swollen with sun, with desire,
those sexy fruits that she loved,

on this radiant All Souls' morning
when she returned to walk with me.

Thum

How many hours
    have I spent on this porch,
                idly stroking my thumb,
        where the trees
join overhead and mingle

their enormous swaying branches.
I want to lie down, my sister said
last fall, *I do not want to eat*,
though her husband and I kept coaxing her
try just half a hemp gummy
in our desperate wish
that her appetite
would magically revive.
	That night she and I watched
The Great British Baking Show,
		second time for both of us,
we sat on their white couch
with her head on my shoulder,
			and once again the Indian guy
		we liked, who found his tray
too heavy, took first prize.
Next morning as her husband
drove me to the airport
		I asked to stop so I could buy
her flowers. I wrote *I love you*
always, and the card stayed
			on their windowsill for weeks
after she died. Tonight I'm
remembering Thum, vile liquid painted on our thumbs
	when we were small,
to make us quit before
we joined our father,
who was stationed in Japan. It tasted bitter,
but bit by bit I'd take it on my tongue
until it wore away,
the bitterness nearly pleasing.
I'm thinking about the strangeness of time,
what fades, what stays,
back then the two small girls
curled up beneath the covers

singing lullabies to each other—
    one now buried in pale linen
on a bed of flowers
in an Amish coffin,
the other possessed
by a nightly dance.
               When I lie down
the cramps begin,
first in the arches of my feet,
    then in my ankles, which torque
and writhe,
and on up until my legs are rigid.
If I can breathe beneath the current
    of agony, sink down beneath
            the agitated waves,
at last the cramps subside.
—And why am I telling you this?
The dance of all this dying,
all this grieving,
all this pain, seems to me
like *prana* moving through us,
like those swaying branches
            in midsummer,
Mississippi, where at night
the vast trees throb with cicadas' silver music.

Little Ole Girl

Averyell Kessler

He spoke to me during the night. In my dreams, I suppose. Although I hadn't heard his voice in many years, I recognized it immediately. It was my late grandfather, Wes. I still remember his gruff words turned soft for me, his misuse of critical pronouns, and his hearty laugh, as well as his ever-present cigar breath and the peppermint aroma of his aftershave. I sit up and scan the darkness. Nothing. Only the faint green nightlight near the bathroom door. There is no sound except the thrum of blood pounding in my ears and the whisper of my own breath. Sleep becomes impossible. Was he here, floating in my dreams or a nightmare of worry and stress? I don't know. I try to forget, but I cannot.

If I close my eyes, I can still see his summer home on Biloxi's Back Bay. If I don't move or turn to glance at a shadow, his wide lawn stretches behind me like a shimmering emerald meadow. If I breathe deeply and allow my mind to blur, a soft breeze drifts over my body, ruffling my hair and swallowing me in the remnants of long-ago years. I stand at the end of his pier, listening to the gentle Gulf rush on shore. In my mind's vivid eye, the sky is an endless canopy of stark blue. A haze of puffball clouds lazes above the water, and Wes' collection of Pride of Mobile azaleas bends heavy with electric pink blossoms. As always, crabs sidle through waves of sea oats picking at tiny bits in the sand. I am a sun brown child, dancing in the water, waiting for Wes to tuck me into the safety of his arms. I look up to see him walking across the lawn, laughing and clapping his hands as I run to greet him. He scoops me up and swings me in a circle. I feel the rough scratch of his beard as he kisses my cheek. "Hey, little ole girl," he says. "What did you do today?" It was the last perfect summer. The last season of quiet accord before everything changed. I returned to Jackson not knowing that I would never visit his home in Biloxi again.

Perfection was shattered early on a school day, barely after sun-up. Mama and I were sharing scrambled eggs and biscuits when Wes knocked on our back door and joined us at the breakfast table. We knew immediately that something was amiss. He was nervous and unshaven, pressing his hands together in a tight knot. He accepted a half full cup of black coffee but did not speak.

"What wrong?" Mama asked.

"Nothing," he replied. His eyes blinked; his head bobbed like a floating cork. Both nervous habits he could not shake. "Um...I..."

"You what?" Mama asked again.

"I ran off an got married," he said. "A lady from Greenwood," he said softly. "Her name's Kate. You'll like her. I hope you'll be friends."

"Where did you meet Kate?"

"At the Stop and Go," Wes replied. The conversation ended and Wes fled faster than a retriever flushing quail.

Within a few short days, Mama realized that Kate's plans did not include friendship. Having stumbled into a complete reversal of fortune, she intended to claim it all.—his love, his attention, and most of all, his fortune. Mama and I stood in the way.

Kate worked steadily over the years, slowly chipping away at our relationship with Wes. Her tactics were predictable, tedious, and unrelenting. Copying my mother's wardrobe down to the last lace handkerchief, squeezing her way into prominent ladies clubs, redecorating Wes' house until it was heavily laden with sterling silver, portraits of her relatives, and lush oriental carpets. Not Wes' style but he shouldered his way through life with Kate and seemed happy enough.

As I eased out of my teen years, Mama dropped to second place, and I became Kate's primary target. Too many interesting things happening to a young woman approaching adulthood. According to Kate, I wasn't paying enough attention to Wes, or following the life plan he'd plotted out for me. In short, I did not obey.

Law school was not on his agenda. When I applied and was accepted, Kate considered it a threat, but also an opportunity. She coached Wes carefully. "She's not listening to you anymore, Wes," Kate said. "Going off all on her own. You're old potatoes, hon. She doesn't need you anymore." A Gallipoli crisis occurred when he attempted to talk me out of it.

"I'm agin' it," he said. "One hundred percent agin' it!"

This was the last time I sat in his office and talked to him face to face. Age did not make him kind. The bullwhip fury of his words drove a spike into my heart and left me sore and trembling. I initiated a separation for my own survival. When he died, I had not spoken to him in over three years.

Now he's back. Or so it seems.

"Hey little ole girl," he said. "Remember me?"

"I'm not allowed to forget," I reply.

"I'm around," he whispers.

"Around?"

"Yes. Around you. All the time."

His voice fades and he is gone. Was he a product of my imagination, or Jacob Marley rising out of an icy doorknocker? He's a fantasy if nothing else, but he reminds me that death does not always mean separation. I remember that I loved him once. Only a little time remains, but enough to heal.

I decide to look again, to measure at my life in inches not

yards; to revive my memories and find Wes as I knew him. Once, he was so dear to me that I believed I had two fathers. Once, I was his little old girl. I will chip away at our wall of separation, one I did not build. I will embroider the things I choose to remember and toss the bad things into a raging trash barrel. Kate will not win again.

I begin with photograph albums from our summers in Biloxi. I see him laughing as we lift a brimming crab net from Back Bay's cloudy water and watch our captives skitter across the pier. In a glossy black and white, I sit in his lap as he lures a curious squirrel closer and closer until it snatches a peanut from his hand. I watch as he picks a handful of cattail fronds and forms them into an imaginary peacock tail. I remember our last perfect summer.

Days pass and I expand my search, shifting through the events of our lives as though they are pages in a mail order catalog. I see him change as hurricane Kate takes hold and I am pushed away. His unhappiness is recorded in vivid portraits snapped on a simple Kodak Brownie. I see his face harden as he ages, not only from years but from the burden of captivity. Why hadn't I noticed? I was too young, I guess. In the last album, I find a photo that blasts our wall of separation into a pile of rubble. He sits on the second row of First Presbyterian Church on my wedding day. I am happy and joyous, as I turn from the altar, holding the arm of my new husband. The organ thunders; the congregation stands. As I pass his pew, I smile and blow him a kiss. Kate's eyes are ice, but tears shine on his cheeks.

As I live out what remains of my September years, I've recovered and made peace. I've forgiven too. Kate has vanished like icicles on a sunny day. Wes is blended so deeply into the circuitry of my brain that we can never be separated. He's around all the time now, urging me forward. He's my inspiration, my encouragement, a source of laughter, and a joyful memory. I do not intend to let him go.

He speaks to me again on a moonless January night. I wake

to the faint aroma of cigar smoke and peppermint. I see noth-ing, but I know he is here.

"Wes?" I whisper. "Are you around?" "Yes," he replies.

"I'm glad," I say.

"I hurt you," he says. "I know better now. Will you forgive me?"

"Already done," I answer.

"When we come, take my hand," he says.

"We? Who's we?"

"You call 'em angels, I call 'em friends. You will too."

"I don't understand, Wes."

"Just take my hand, little ole girl," he says. "I'll always be around, even at the end. No one goes home alone."

When a Mother Leaves Her Child

Angela Jackson-Brown

In loving memory of Gwendolyn Pendleton

No matter how old you are, you want her to stay. Even if your face has been kissed with wrinkles; even If your hair has thinned or white strands have begun to outnumber the darker hairs of your youth;
even if you walk a little slower and your back is slightly bent;
even if you, too, are a parent or a grandparent;
you never want your mother to leave.

You never stop wanting your mother's embrace. You never stop wanting your mother's words of wisdom. You never stop wanting to hear her tell you she loves you. You never stop wanting her warm breath against your face. You never stop wanting to climb into her lap and have her rock you into a gentle sleep. You never stop wanting your mother.

When your mother finally does go away,
that part of your heart that belonged to her and her alone,
crumbles just a little. You think at any moment
you too might leave, that the pain of her absence

might be enough to take you out too, but inside you hear
her whisper,
It's not your time. You must stay and know that
even though I'm gone, I'm not really gone.

You hear her say to you: *See your eyes, those eyes are*
mine looking back at you. See that smile, that is my smile
on your precious face. Listen to that laugh, that's all mine too.
I'm with you, she says, *even when I'm not, because you are me,*
and I am you.

Death is merely a bridge that we must cross over,
and although it feels like we are separated from those we love
we aren't, not really, because pieces of those we love will
always dwell inside of us. Parts of them leave, but the parts
that matter, their undying love, remain as long as we have memory and breath.

So, mothers never truly leave their children when they die,
because their love lives on for all eternity.

Poems About Parents and Grief

Lauren Camp

I wish I didn't have to write about grief, but grief has been
a powerful muse. I hold my parents close—through detail
and memory—as I shape the words in each poem.

Prayer for My Father's Frontal Lobes

Leave him a little, the prelude to night. Leave him
his languages and lonesome embellishments. First name
and leave him a gap to last strip

of being. We redistrict to his breakings, and he to old pho-
tographs with content. Leave him far more—

the wide anchor of winter, his eye on the flat of the river.
The desert is blooming

its nests and mending. These days I confide in vague frac-
tions, the durable light.

Leave him the ordinary.
Leave him his storms. Pray away vanishing.

Goodbye to Aggressions and Generous Gestures

Every visit he didn't and didn't and then could
able less. This was an extravagant

minimum we'd come to expect. Winter is endless

tight branches. I remember his voice as a nation, all the doors
shutting and us eating
our behaviors. Sorry citizens. Evenings, the street
                              loosed out my small windows.
              Name something that seems perfect.

I'm telling you my father's silence, every mobbing of it. Not
telling the clamor for days of unused parts
of our hope. Kafka wrote *A cage went in search of a bird.*

I don't know if I'm lonely.
Name the doorway, then walk through.

Not to tongue more than he can, I hurry to listen. With vanishing,
He has removed each pronoun of home. He still wants
                      to name
                              Swerve and siege, pause and anthem.

I sit beside him in the thrift and watch it froth.
Love is a habit. Then a moon. A spatter
of color priming the treetops. I laugh about the moon. He laughs.

When he laughs, there is so much
of him—multiple pieces: and, of, or, if. What are our names?

The lock, the solution. Name it all.

A Precise Small Thing

I didn't know I would run out of time to memorize
your voice. After three days trying, I just now remember the
name of a trombonist I heard three years ago,

and you have been missing 3,322 days.

Dad laughed when I asked for the recording of you saying *no one is home right now* with your wine-sopped, grass-pure voice. I can't remember it at all, that voice.

Not the strange wide way you had of stretching Ws or the laugh that started from a precise small thing and rolled on and on, expanding into time
we didn't realize was ending.

Or the way you called to us, your voice becoming
a near shriek in the almost dark, our names as large as puppets expected to move back into that box of home again.

Or how you said *Dad*. Just that one word. How you cried at the supper table some nights your voice turning into salt and red breath.

How you moaned gently. How your voice in my hands expired into something I could no longer hear, something smaller than atoms.

A Hundred Cigarettes

Cathy Smith Bowers

for Rosi

Are you a smoker? the physician's assistant
asked, filling out the pre-procedure form
for my latest colonoscopy. *No*, I was quick

to answer, *since the smoking I did so long
ago in college couldn't possibly count.* It
was then she looked me in the eye, as if

conducting some criminal investigation: *Did
you smoke a hundred cigarettes?* I sat stunned,
wondering why in the world I would have

counted the exact number of cigarettes I
had smoked in my life. A hundred? Hell,
it took me that many just to get through *Moby*

Dick alone. And how could I deny all those
post-sex drags I sucked into my lungs
when I should have been at home in bed

with *Elmer Gantry* or *Ethan Frome*? Oh,
Rosi, I can only imagine the delight you
would have taken had you been there when

she asked that crazy question. Laughing
your silly head off. You who busted me
to Mama too many years ago to count

while you kept smoking one right after
the other until you died. So it is you I think of
now as I lie fetalled, waiting for the anesthesia

to kick finally in. For the procedure your
too-soon death set long ago in motion. That
every semi-decade saves my life again.

A hundred cigarettes. A hundred prayers
to you, my little turncoat sister. And all
the hundred ways I miss you still.

A Brother Dying

Nancy Dorman-Hickson

"You have to come," Doug implores on the phone. "I can't deal with him any longer." While Doug was at work, my brother Dennis had wandered into a nearby busy intersection, stretched out on the pavement, and waited to die. Someone, a neighbor or a passing motorist, called the police. An ambulance carted my brother to the hospital. "He's home now," his friend says. "But you have to come."

I leave Birmingham and arrive in Denver the next night. Doug leads me into the tiny cluttered bedroom where Dennis lay.

My brother's eyes are glassy, his skin flushed, his body rail-thin, almost but not quite the emaciated skeleton of TV drama. Since the last time I saw him, his HIV-status has become full-blown AIDS.

"Nancy, you came to see me," Dennis says. He smiles. I lean over to hug him. "Wait!" he cries. "Put on the gloves. Don't touch me until you put on the gloves." Alarmed, I back away and leave the room to consult Doug, a nurse. There is no need for gloves, he assures me. "He gets...confused," he says, shaking his head.

I walk back into the dimly lit room where Dennis rests on a twin bed. His small body seems lost amid the books, papers, clothes, dishes, and electronic equipment crammed into the room. Suddenly his arm flails in the air, puppet-stringed by synapses that have no business firing. The thing he most feared about his illness has come to pass; the disease has invaded his brain. After a few moments of this silent posturing, Dennis notices. "I'm exercising," he offers and grins, a polite explanation for the inexplicable. It is a small, if macabre, glimmer of his past boyish charm.

A tarnished silver-backed mirror lies on the bed beside him. He picks it up and gazes at his reflection, grinning at the ghastly image staring back. "Don't I look good?" he asks. I don't answer. He insists. "Don't I look good?"

"Yes, Dennis," I lie. Later I learn the mirror is constantly within his reach. It seems to reassure him that he is still within the physical realm. I try to carry on a conversation but his concentration is non-existent. The fever takes him in and out of consciousness. He looks hollow. I don't think he has the energy to sustain life for long. I call our family in Mississippi and give them my assessment.

Dennis' rapid recovery the next morning confounds me, as does everything about this baffling Jekyll-and-Hyde disease. He is weak but he wants to eat and take a bath. Later, he grabs a heavy box and carts it upstairs as if it is nothing.

Despite Dennis' improvement, Doug's mind remains unchanged. He won't—no *can't*—care for Dennis any longer. Doug is a friend, nothing more, and has no real obligation to Dennis.

That night when I lie in a borrowed bed next to my brother's room, I imagine that I feel my own heart slow and speed, speed and slow, synching with my sibling's faltering pulse. Worry fuels my mind, keeping me from sleep. An earlier conversation I had with my older sister taunts me. "Dennis will want to move in with you but Mark won't let him," Beth said. It's true, my husband doesn't want the burden of a sick person, especially one to whom he has never been close. But even without Mark's objections, I know I am too weak to take in Dennis and watch him suffer. Living with guilt seems the lesser of two evils.

With Doug's disavowal of responsibility, I drown in a sea of uncertainty. I am the soother in the family; I am not the decision maker.

My younger sister calls. "Do you want me to come?" Merrie asks.

"If you want to," I reply. I cannot admit I need help.

She ferrets out a response from me, nonetheless. "No, I am asking you," she insists. "Do you want me to come?"

"Yes," I croak the words. I am both resentful and grateful that she has forced me to say it aloud.

When Dennis was first diagnosed, his search for painless cures ran parallel to the various painkillers he sought all of his life. EST, recreational drug use, and the path to reincarnation via Shirley MacLaine were replaced over time with visualization, positive energy, and a macrobiotic diet. To be young, male, gay, and Mississippian requires looking for salvation in unlikely places.

During the next few days, Dennis' renewed strength continues to rally.

"I want to stay here with Doug," he says.

"That isn't an option," I say quietly.

"I'll go home to Daddy's," he says.

"I'll ask," I reply. "But you know you two have never gotten along."

"I want to go home with you," he says.

I say nothing. I begin to cry.

"Okay, okay, I'll go to Heaven," Dennis says, patting me on the arm.

He is not referring to the Great Beyond but to a nearby celestially named commune in the Rockies. When he visited there previously, Heaven's "angels" fed him the same sinful lie he had told himself. *Why, yes, Dennis, you're right*, they said. *You don't have to die. Death is a choice; you don't have to choose it.* He believed their doctrine—right up until the time they informed him he wouldn't be allowed to work in the kitchen anymore.

"They told me it made the other people nervous when I handled the food," he tells me now, his voice cracking at the telling of one more flawed path to salvation.

When my sister arrives from North Carolina, we go in together to tell Dennis we have found a nearby hospice for him. "It is in a house, Dennis, just a few blocks from Doug's, so he can visit you," I tell him.

"But why?" he protests. "I'm better."

It's true. I have no response.

My sister grasps his hand; she is crying. "Dennis, we want to do what's best for you," she pleads, perhaps trying to convince herself as much as our brother. Ever practical, Merrie has never been swayed by Dennis' charm, his imagination, and his stories that dazzle. But she is clearly moved by love today.

He, too, is affected by our stalwart sister's emotion. "Okay, I'll go," he says. I recognize his resignation as an act of love. From his perspective he is giving up his freedom to accommodate our hobgoblin needs. He thinks he isn't going to die. I wish once again I had the courage and the wherewithal to take him home with me.

At the hospice, he has his own room and bath. He asks one of the nurses if he can do his own laundry. "Yes, or the staff can do it for you," she chirps.

"Can I make my own food?" he asks. Within reason, she tells him. "But you might like our food," she adds.

He looks at the locks on the doors leading to the outside world. His eyebrows rise.

"We have drugs here," she rushes to explain.

He isn't buying it. "Can I leave?" he asks.

She pauses. "Yes, if someone accompanies you."

He sinks down on the bed at the answer, defeated. It is, as he suspected, a prison. I quell my rush of empathic frustration. I remind myself that this is the same person who lay down in the middle of a busy road just a few days ago. Like a shield, I hold in front of me that image and the other events that have led us to this place. But my attempts at constructing a protective barrier for my guilt are pierced by the more immediate, monstrous reality. The hospice's cheerful décor and perky staff try, but the place nonetheless whispers death at every turn. "In loving memory" plaques line the walls. The other hospice residents are old and confined to bed. They wait. They breathe pure oxygen and the aroma of sweet flowers and wait.

Dennis, on the other hand, is well enough to have a friend bring him a stationary bike. He breathes in the sweat of his own efforts and schemes of peddling his way back into life.

The facility's case manager insists Dennis, Merrie, and I settle Dennis' funeral plans. I try to explain to her that Dennis is still denying the inevitable, that his denial seems to be fueling his strength to keep going. "What is the harm in letting him keep his fantasy?" I implore.

She doesn't respond and I realize I have failed to convince her when Dennis enters the room and she begins asking him ghoulish questions. What funeral home does he prefer? Does he want to be cremated? I feel like I am in the room with Nurse Ratchet from *One Flew Over the Cuckoo's Nest.*

Dennis, on the other hand, responds gently to her invasive questions. "I am not dying," he says softly. "I'm getting stronger." He looks at all of us. "I shouldn't be here." I don't meet his eyes.

Perhaps it is only the circumstances that grant me the temporary gift of prophecy. When a hospice worker knocks on the door during our meeting, I shudder. I know somehow the phone call for my sister is about her boy. When she left her seven-month-old son with our stepmother in Mississippi, he had been slightly sick. The "virus" he had when Merrie flew to Denver has been diagnosed as an intestinal blockage, requiring immediate surgery.

She is crying again, on the verge of sheer panic at this latest blow. "I have to go to him," Merrie says to us. She turns to Dennis, "I'm sorry. But he's my first priority."

"He will be all right," Dennis responds, hugging her, rubbing her back. "He will be all right." In an instant, he has gone from fending off funeral arrangements to comforting our distraught sister. They both cry and hold each other tightly. I am dry-eyed, too shocked to assimilate this new tragedy.

When I call to make my sister's airline reservations, the woman in charge of family emergency rates asks if the situation is life or death. "God, I hope not," I blurt. It's then I realize how I've been fending off my own thoughts of funeral arrangements, those in my mind for my baby nephew. I fall apart and begin crying.

"I hope not, too, dear," she says. When I hear the caring note in her voice, I begin to sob in earnest. I am reduced to depending on the kindness of strangers, a Blanche Dubois runaway in Denver.

My sister leaves and I return to my brother. The hospice has a room for family members to stay overnight. Instead, I spend penance on the floor in Dennis' room, my hand stretched to his in supplication throughout the night. A nurse comes in and fusses about this arrangement. "We have a room for you," she tsks. I lash out at her. It feels good to release biting words. I am so angry.

"Dennis has to learn to deal with us himself," another hospice worker tells me the next morning. "You mustn't run interference for him. It will be better if he gets used to our routine." The reasonable side of me knows she is right. But that part of me that has always been Dennis' soul mate rages insanely. Why should my brother, who has lived his entire life rebelling, have to conform just so he can die?

I need not have worried. Dennis did what came naturally: he resisted. Just as Merrie's child grew stronger every day after the surgery, so too did Dennis continue to get healthier after we condemned him to die.

"I'm out," he says to me after I returned home. He is calling to tell me the news of how he "escaped" the hospice. I can practically hear the grin on his face. "I got an apartment."

I want to cheer with him: *Yes, Death, go to hell.* I give only token protest about his change in venue. A voice in my head reminds me that, left to his own devices, he was mentally unbalanced enough to try death-by-passing-motorist a few weeks ago. I stifle it.

For a while, his phone calls are more coherent, filled with his day-to-day happenings. The home health people bring "yucky" meals but he likes the visits. Doug or other friends drive him to the clinic on days he has appointments. When he feels well enough, he walks to the park a few blocks away.

It must have been on one of these trips to the park that the stranger saw him. Apparently, Dennis looked so forlorn, the man, also HIV-positive, was moved to take my brother in and care for him. I burn with shame that a stranger did what I did not. I'll carry shame about that decision until I die.

Not long afterward, the good Samaritan calls. "Dennis is really sick," he says. "You need to come." This time my stepmother joins me on the trip to Denver. While gliding past pink clouds and purple mountains, I recall overlapping moments of my life with my brother's.

In the early 1970s, I knew all the cool music long before any of my peers. At age twelve, I was a junior hippie, riding around in a brown Pinto with Led Zepplin, ZZ Top, and Edgar Winter blaring. Dennis, a long-haired hippie in earnest, was in the driver's seat. He never seemed to mind having me around.

He was always more than my big brother. He was my confidante. I was a much-too-adult kid, with no one with whom to share my alienating fears. Except Dennis. He listened. It helped to know that there was no way I could shock him. He was always one up on me in the shock department.

I remember just after my mother died when I confessed that I had thought about killing myself. "If you do, I will too," Dennis fiercely told me. His passion convinced me he meant every word. It was a brilliant reverse suicide pact; I believed him and refrained.

He could be manipulative and selfish, working circumstances to suit him. But he was also genuinely charming and kind hearted. I'll never forget when he came to visit me after we were both grown and living separate lives. I sighed and smiled indulgently at the sight of my big brother getting off the plane. His hair was past his shoulders and he wore an outrageous costume of purple and pink pants, tank top, and Jesus sandals. We walked over to the rental car booth where the matronly clerk gave him a withering disdainful look.

Dennis just smiled and began talking. Within a few minutes, I could almost read the woman's thoughts. *Why, he's just a little boy*, she smiled, *just a scruffy little boy.*

Once, when I visited him, a rather large woman friend of his was there. I commented on the unusual color of her sweatshirt. It was the yellow of a #2 pencil. She and Dennis began to giggle.

"What's funny?" I asked.

"Dennis said I looked like a school bus," she replied, laughing again. It would have been cruel coming from someone else. But somehow Dennis' candor never offended. He knew how to assess people and what he could get away with.

My reverie ends when the plane touches down in Denver. When my stepmother arrives, we take a rental car to Dennis' new home. I try to prepare myself mentally for what we will find.

"Nancy, you came to see me!" Dennis says, the same glad cry of greeting as before. This time he does not mention gloves nor do his arms contort in wild posturing. But now his skeletal form is the undeniable picture of walking death. Auschwitz comes to mind. It isn't his barely papered bones that sear me the most, however.

"What did you do to your hair?" I blurt. His once golden locks are now a dull grayish brown, the unnatural color of chocolate candy gone bad.

"Nothing," he replies, puzzled. I kick myself for being thoughtless and pray he does not still have a mirror fixation.

But the pain has moved him beyond such trivial matters.

A portrait of Jesus that he had at Doug's house hangs over

his bed. "He believes in Jesus," my father has said, comforted by the presence of the cheap painting when he visited Dennis days earlier. My father—a conservative Christian, Republican, life-time member of the VFW, for God's sake—has never come close to understanding his only son's life. He loves him as best he can, but he doesn't understand him.

It is true, Dennis has taken to talking about Jesus. "Jesus loves me, doesn't he?" he asks now, his fever making his voice as high-pitched as a child's. The dementia magnifies his sweetness, his child-like nature. Like our dad, I, too, take comfort in remembered scripture about blessed little children entering the kingdom of God and childhood prayers "Now I lay me down to sleep..."

Dennis wakes up and without hesitation, as if he has been waiting, asks the lone question I dread the most.

"Am I dying?" It is the pure, innocent question of a child asking his mother about some wonder, some puzzling riddle to be solved by someone he trusts. It's a cosmic question that requires honesty.

"Yes," I whisper, extinguishing the last flicker in the fantasy he—and, to some extent, I have breathed life into since his diagnosis.

He closes his eyes, sighing deeply. "Okay," he whispers, "Okay." Then he opens his eyes again and ventures a step further: "Is it going to hurt?"

"God, I hope not," I blurt. "I don't think so."

He mulls this over in the muddy river that is now his mind, then throws out a life preserver, that of his paper-thin hand, toward the only salvation we mere mortals can ever hope to give each other.

"Will you love me?" he asks.

A drowning woman, I cling desperately to his hand. "Yes, I will love you." I feel the weak pulse of his hand in mine and, out of habit, try to will it to match the stronger rhythm of my own. Trying to save him continues to be my involuntary reflex, my flailing arms from the faulty thinking of misfired synapses.

He falls asleep with me clutching his hand. I rock back and forth, back and forth, and pray voicelessly, mindlessly, "God, God, God, don't let it hurt."

When he wakes up again, he glances down, startled to find my hand still anchored in his. "Oh, I forgot. I forgot you were loving me."

I am rock-sure of what to answer: "I will always love you," I promise. "I will never forget to love you."

This answer pleases him. He rewards me with a peaceful smile and closes his eyes to rest.

My Grandfather, My Angel

The Rev. Joanna J. Seibert M.D.

It is rare that I still do not think about my grandfather at some point during my day. He taught me about unconditional love. No, my grandfather *was* unconditional love. In addition, I know he also saved my life on at least three occasions.

I grew up in a small tidewater town in Virginia where the York River is birthed by the union of the Mattaponi and the Pamunky Rivers. My two maternal grandparents lived on Third Street. My parents, my younger brother, and I lived on Second Street. I usually saw my grandparents at some time during each day growing up.

Before I could read, my grandfather would sit me down and read me the funny papers each Sunday before lunch. I was mesmerized as he made each small story come to life.

He also bought a farm across from my hometown on the Mattaponi River before I was school age. The farmhouse was an old plantation house built in the 1770s. I would sit with my grandfather in a swing on the porch, which ran across the whole front of the house, as he answered all my most important questions about life. Why did my mother make me take naps? When would I be too old for my mother to give me a spanking? Was Santa Claus real? When I spent the night, I had my own room on the second floor up the stairs wide enough for three people to walk beside each other. This front bedroom seemed massive with two tall dormer windows with window seats. When I learned to read, I would curl up with my favorite book in the window and imagine what my life would be like in the future after I had grown up, so to speak. I knew one thing. My grandparents would always be beside me.

The first time my grandfather saved my life was when we were swimming in the Mattaponi River next to his farm. He had taught me how to swim, and I know I was a good swimmer because I would later swim for hours along the shoreline. This near-miss tragedy occurred when I was early primary school age, and I have no definite recollection why I suddenly could not stay above water. I think it was high tide, and I had unconsciously gone out beyond the dock where the water was now over my head and panicked when I could not touch the bottom. My grandfather quickly rushed to my side and swam me to shore. I remember later he told me that he as well would have drowned trying to rescue me if he had not been able to save me. I remembered much later how that best described to me the depth of his love.

Growing up, I remember my exact routine on Sundays. First, I went to the Methodist church with my mother. We then had Sunday dinner at my grandparents. It was the same meal—iced tea, fried chicken, potato salad, green beans, homemade rolls made by my grandmother's cook, Mabel, followed by Mabel's rich pound cake for dessert. After my grandparents took a nap, we visited my grandmother's relatives who lived close by, often down dirt country roads. I also remember some homes in the country even had dirt floors, and most had outhouses. Next, we went to my grandparent's farm, where my grandfather took me for walks in the woods and taught me about the trees and plants, and snakes. We then went back to my grandparent's house in town and walked to services at the Baptist church a block away. I loved to sit beside my grandfather on about the third row on the right and hear him loudly sing the very moving old Baptist hymns. I think his favorite was "Amazing Grace," which actually is an Anglican hymn! But I never mentioned that. On special Sunday nights at the end of the service, I would look forward to the drama of a baptism that unfolded in the sunken full immersion font in the very front of the church behind the large pulpit. We then walked back to my grandparents' house, where we had Seven Up ice cream floats and watched the Ed Sullivan Show. I spent the night in what seemed like the most enormous bed I had ever seen, in my grandparent's front guest room. I got up on Monday morning and, after breakfast, walked the short nine blocks to school.

My grandfather was a watchmaker and had a jewelry store between his house and my school on Main Street across from the Farmers and Merchant Bank. Every day after school, on my way home, I would walk to my grandfather's store. He would give me a nickel to go one store down to Riddle's Drug Store to buy my favorite ice cream cone. If I had friends with me, they received a nickel for ice cream as well.

My grandmother and I would sometimes help my grandfather out in the store on Saturdays, showing china, crystal, and jewelry out of tall glass cases that came up to my chest. Of course, the store was busier on Saturdays when the farmers and their families came to town. But, I mostly loved to look across the counters and watch my grandfather intently trying to repair someone's priceless timepiece that was more important than time. My grandfather was a tall, handsome man with thick wavy black hair. I always thought he looked like Ezio Pinza, the Metropolitan Opera singer who sang in *South Pacific* with Mary Martin on Broadway. At work, he sat on a tall stool next to the large display window at the front of his store, where he had better light. On a wall behind his work desk was a large wooden board with watches on cup hocks with white tags defining their owners and their present state of repair.

Alas, all of this now seems like a lost art. If our watch doesn't work, we throw it away! I want to tell people, "Wait, my grandfather can fix your watch!"

My favorite holiday is the fourth of July, maybe because of what my grandparents planned when I was growing up. All of my grandmother's relatives came out of the woodwork for a huge Smith family reunion at my grandparents' farm. I was in charge of the name tags. After the guests arrived, I remember sitting on a short stool churning ice cream freezers until the handles would not move. The freezers then took a place of honor down steep stairs into the cool dark cellar under the house until dessert time. This was one of the few times I was allowed in the cellar.

We ate the usual homemade picnic foods by the river, including fried chicken, corn on the cob, corn pudding, potato salad, biscuits, slaw, baked beans, deviled eggs, Jell-O salads, and watermelon as we stood next to two long tall tables my grandfather had made. At night we sang, told family stories, and filled ourselves with more pie and ice cream and cake until dark. I do not remember fireworks. However, I will never forget one night. For some reason, a few months earlier, I had decided I wanted to learn how to play the accordion. I think an accordion teacher had started coming to West Point from Richmond one day a week. My grandfather bought a small one for me and paid for the lessons. That night my grandfather went and took the accordion out of its case and strapped it to me. Then, to everyone's surprise, he lifted me up on the table as I played "On Top of Old Smoky," the first and only piece I had learned so far. This was also about my grandfather's birthplace in the Smoky Mountains. I can still feel the delight we both had that evening. I knew he was proud of my accomplishment. I was as well. I had no idea that I was capable of doing something like that.

Without saying, Christmas was always very special at my grandparents'. I would go with my grandfather over to his farm to cut down a small cedar tree to put on top of my grandmother's marble-topped table in their front living room of their town house where they lived in the winter. My grandmother put me totally in charge of decorating the tree and her home. I remember the multicolored lights of red, orange, blue bulbs much too big for the small tree. I would skillfully hide the hot lights as close to the trunk and major branches, so they had a mystical effect. I always went overboard with tinsel, never thrown, carefully placed. My brother and I would open our presents at home as early as possible on Christmas Day. We always knew Christmas was still not over as we looked forward to even more gifts to open soon at my grandparents' before Christmas dinner. My uncle—my mother's brother—and his wife, who were childless, would be there and would always give us some exotic gifts. I can't remember what I was given, but I remember the Christmas they gave my younger brother a relatively large canon complete with caps! As we opened presents, my grandfather tossed the wrapping paper in handfuls into a roaring fire that burned larger and brighter. Sometimes it seemed the chimney might explode. The miniature grandfather clock over his mantle would also shake. I remember those times often as I pass by that same clock in a place of honor in our den.

When I went away to college and medical school and residency, my grandfather wrote to me at least once a week on his old typewriter with a used ribbon. He had taught himself in his business to type rapidly with two fingers. Almost every sentence ended with etc. etc. He frequently hit the key next to the one he wanted, making reading his letters a fun word-solving adventure, especially with the ribbon on its last leg. Besides news from home, his letters were filled with stories of his life in World War I. The Army had been his formal education. He wanted me to know what he had learned about his new life and new relationships, sometimes in times of great difficulty in the world outside of a sheltered home. Included in every letter was a dollar bill. When I was in college in North Carolina, girls on my hall would come and gather around my bed and listen to my grandfather's letters. Maybe they were missing a grandfather. For some, it was helping me to learn how to decipher the words.

For others, they may have missed small-town life. A few history majors may have been interested in the First World War stories.

The dreaded call came from my mother not long after starting my job as a pediatric radiologist at the very infancy of an Arkansas Children's Hospital shortly after we came to Little Rock. I had not lived near my grandparents for almost twenty years, but I was devastated. "Your grandfather is unconscious and not talking or moving." I flew back to Virginia and rode with my mother to the small community hospital. When I walked into the room, my grandfather looked over at the door. He sat up in bed, opened his eyes wide, loudly gasped, and then just as quickly lay back down with his eyes closed. He never spoke or made any sign of recognition again. I sat helpless at his bedside.

I had no idea what to do next. Then, something brought to my memory the times my grandfather read to me as a child. Just before leaving home in Little Rock, I had a nudge to pack in my bag a little-used *Book of Common Prayer*. That morning at the hospital, I did remember that my grandfather often quoted the Psalms. So, I pulled the prayer book out and quietly started reading the Psalms almost at the back of the book. Initially, I was embarrassed and read more softly when hospital personnel or my mother walked in on me. But soon, I lived totally in those last moments, oblivious to the outside world, being with someone I loved who had taught me what it was to be loved. There were only two of us sharing love together in the present moment that we thought might be for the last time. I knew with all my heart, mind, and soul that my grandfather heard every word I spoke. Even today, as I read those first Psalms, I am immediately carried back to my grandfather's small hospital room where one lies, and the other sits as if "they are like trees planted by streams of water, bearing fruit in due season, with leaves that do not wither; everything they do shall prosper." (Psalm 1:3 *Book of Common Prayer* (*BCP*, p. 585.) I hoped my grandfather would forgive me when I read the Psalms from the *BCP* rather than the Bible in the King James Version.

A week or so later, I returned for his funeral shortly after his ninety-first birthday. It was an open casket service, which so bothered me as being disrespectful of the dead and a spectacle for the curious living. I do not remember the service, but I can remember crying without embarrassment at the service in the same Baptist church where I sat between my grandparents on Sunday nights, often with my grandfather's arm over my shoulder. At the family and friends gathering afterwards at my parent's home, I remember my uncle, my grandfather's son, humorously asking me why I, a grown woman, loudly cried at the funeral. I have no idea what I said, but I do remember I couldn't understand why someone would question that.

During the next few days, I knew I had to do something to honor my grandfather's life. He rarely was critical of my behavior, even during the time of my divorce in medical school, but he often gently told me he was praying that I would stop smoking cigarettes. His mother had died a respiratory death from tuberculosis when he was five years old. He must have remembered something about that kind of death. I had twenty pack-years of smoking. I decided to honor him by quitting smoking. I had tried several times but without long-standing success. Finally, I quit smoking to honor my grandfather. It soon became a spiritual experience. I have not had a cigarette since my grandfather's funeral, December 7, 1979. This is the second time my grandfather saved my life. My younger brother died five years ago of complications from smoking, and I could have so easily done the same.

It has been over forty years since that day of my grandfather's funeral. I remembered becoming overwhelmed in my medical studies and practice. While raising a family over the years, I had stopped being involved in a spiritual life. However, My Christian upbringing taught me about resurrection and the possibility of again being with those we loved in the resurrection. I had to believe that and live that. I had to believe I would, in some manner, be with my grandparents again. So, after at least fifteen years, I returned to the Episcopal Church, which I had joined in medical school during my divorce. At the time, I felt like a bad person. No one in my family had been divorced before, even though many should have. However, the Dean of St. Mary's Cathedral in Memphis, William Dimmick, welcomed me and reconnected me to the God of love.

Now on my second journey back to the church, I learned about a whole new way of living for myself and my family. If we are talking about being saved, I believe that I was saved on Good Friday when Jesus taught us about sacrificial love and led us to a new life in the resurrection. However, I do believe my grandfather saved me again by leading me in his death to a life built on the unconditional love of God towards us and each other. In turn, this leads us out of ourselves to love unconditionally in the world, as my grandfather had once taught me. Through my grandfather, I learned that God never gives up on us and, like the "hound of heaven," constantly calls us back to be connected to God and God's unconditional love. I am counting this as the third time my grandfather saved my life.

Several years ago, I became interested in our genealogy. This is most certainly a sign of getting old. I soon became intrigued about my grandfather's birthplace and home growing up deep in the Smoky Mountains. He had twenty brothers and sisters. His father had three wives, and we believe his father also ran a grocery store. My grandfather's mother was a second wife and died when he was five years old. He only had one full sister, Mary. The Great Smoky Mountains National Park took over their home, so it was hard to find and visit. In my studies of our family heritage, I did find, however, a great treasure. It was a possible location of where my grandfather's mother was buried. A few years ago, my husband and my daughter helped me make the trek to my great-grandmother's possible grave in an isolated graveyard deep into the forest of the Great Smoky Mountains National Park. We had stopped there as we were making a trip back to Virginia. It was not an easy adventure, especially since

I had many mobility issues and walked with difficulty with a cane at the time. Presently I am now on a walker. We entered the Park outside of Gatlinburg, went over a tiny bridge on a dirt road, then an even smaller bridge, parked on a road with a chain across it, followed a stream for a half-mile on an uneven path with roots crisscrossing it until we came to the secret, well-kept cemetery. It was a cathedral-like open space framed by a canopy of trees. I could never have made it without my husband making a path ahead of us as our daughter walked right beside me. My grandfather's mother's gravestone was immediately recognizable. It was one of the tallest and right next to an identical monument for my grandfather's father's first wife.

This adventure into the Great Smoky Mountains became one of many ways I continue to honor my grandfather. Working with people in my church who grieve the death of a loved one, I have learned that honoring the relationship is the best way to live through the grief. I think this is one more thing my grandfather taught me or is teaching me as well. So again, the unconditional love of my grandfather led me to reach out to others, especially the grieving, who are so often needing to know what unconditional love is all about and that it is still present in their lives. This is the only way we hold on to that kind of love. It is a paradox. We keep the love by giving it away.

I know my grandfather was not perfect. He had definite opinions about things. I know he did not always get along with his employees. He and his son were somewhat estranged. I think it was because my uncle thought he loved my mother better. As a result, we could all write a book about family systems and family dynamics. I say this to remind myself that my grandfather was not God and often missed the mark in relationships. But today, what I remember is his love. He taught me about love that does not require something back, unconditional love. My grandfather saved my life at least three times and brought me back to God, the source of unconditional love in my attempt to stay in a relationship with my grandfather after his death.

Doing so allowed me to know what love is like "with skin on," and then share it, and give it away, just as he did.

I so often feel my grandparent's presence with me. This most often occurs when I am able to accomplish things I never thought I could do, like playing "On Top of Old Smoky" on the accordion on top of a picnic table in the dark!

Some might call my grandfather an angel sent by God to care for and love a young girl with no sense of self-value. But, even more, I would call my grandfather an icon of unconditional love, loving me no matter what I did or accomplished.

I also think I forgot to tell you that I am named after my grandfather and grandmother. His name was Joe, and her name was Anna. We also named our daughter Joanna. Our middle son, John, who practices medicine in middle Tennessee not too far from where my grandfather grew up, carries my grandfather's last name, Whaley, as his middle name. John is the only one carrying on the family name since my grandfather's only son had no children. I am learning from my grandfather that a memory can be just as important as a name.

And so, I write to each of you to carry on my grandfather's memory as the Spirit moves you in your own memory.

Hitting the Wall

Susan Cushman

On the wall just outside the entrance to the Mississippi Sports Hall of Fame and Museum in Jackson, Mississippi, there's a single monument dedicated to my father—the man known as "The Guru of Running" in Mississippi. Etched in marble, the image of 67-year-old Bill Johnson, wearing a Mississippi State University baseball cap and a white running singlet, stands above the names of the winners of the "Watermelon 5K," the race which he founded in 1982. Under his name are the dates of his birth and death: January 20, 1930—July 9, 1998.

Even seasoned marathon runners often experience "hitting the wall" around mile twenty of the 26.219-mile race. Dad taught the runners he mentored during his career about this experience, explaining how the body runs out of chemical energy and the runner can suddenly feel as though his shoes are full of lead. He was able to avoid this during many of the marathons he ran, with proper nutrition and training.

My father's athletic career didn't begin with running. At Mississippi State University in the late '40s and early '50s he was the starting pitcher on the baseball team—including the first year State won the SEC championship—and also lettered in golf and basketball. After a brief stint on a farm league in Florida in the late '40s, he gave up baseball and became a championship level golfer, winning the City of Jackson (Mississippi) and numerous country club invitationals throughout the state during the '50s and '60s. When he could no longer play scratch golf, (always shooting par or better) he turned in his cleats for running shoes. Dad had been a smoker for twenty-five years, and after quitting in the early '70s, he knew he needed to do something to keep the weight off. Both his parents had died of heart attacks, so Dad set out on a path of low-fat eating and intensive aerobic exercise.

He traded his two-martini business lunches for noonday runs with a group of men at the YMCA. This was before the running craze hit, so everyone said they were "hog wild" about running, and they eventually became known as the "Hog Wilds" and even had running shirts printed with that insignia. By the end of the '70s Dad was running 5Ks, 10Ks, and even marathons. He was only fifty-two years old when he retired from the life insurance business and opened "Bill Johnson's Phidippides Sports," a retail business specializing in athletic shoes, clothes, and informal training advice.

Life was good for Bill Johnson for the next fifteen years. From 1982 to 1997 he enjoyed a healthy lifestyle and a successful business. He ran all the big marathons, like Boston and New York, several times. One year he even competed in a triathlon. All this after age 50. Wanting to include the family, he built an aerobic dance studio adjacent to his store, which my mother oversaw. I taught aerobics there from 1982 until 1988, when I moved away from Jackson, and those were without a doubt the healthiest years of my life. To say Dad was a positive role model to those around him would be an understatement. Six-foot-two, with a slim runner's body, sky blue eyes and a mischievously dimpled smile (he always reminded me of Clint Eastwood), he seemed invincible. But all that changed abruptly in 1997.

The Marathon Begins

Well, it actually started changing in 1995, when Dad first told his physician that he felt something strange, a twinge when he took a deep breath. Early chest x-rays showed a small, vague, gray area, but the bronchoscopy and needle biopsy were negative, so the doctors weren't concerned. But a life-long athlete is so attuned to his body that he can pick up signs others miss, so Dad went back again and again, asking for more x-rays. By 1997 the gray area proved to be a malignant tumor, bigger than any wall he had ever hit running marathons.

The next fourteen months were trying times for our family. Dad went into the hospital on May 13, 1997, expecting to have only one lobe of his right lung removed. During the surgery, a 4.5-centimeter adenocarcinoma with metastatic disease was found in one lobe, with involvement of a lymph node. A 5-millimeter lesion was discovered in another lobe, which also had metastasized. Additionally, a third tumor "of long duration" was found. The surgeon performed a pneumonectomy—the removal of his entire right lung—but unfortunately he wasn't able to completely eradicate the metastatic process that had begun to invade Dad's body.

Bill Johnson entered surgery a seasoned athlete and came out a semi-invalid. He would never again drive a car. In a few months he would no longer be able to take slow walks around an indoor track. He would become confined to a wheelchair and would require a portable oxygen tank at all times. Most people would have caved under such an emotional glycogen depletion, but Dad's training as a runner, combined with the community's image of him as hero—not only in athletics, but also in the spiritual and civic worlds—kept him from bonking at the twenty-mile marker of his final marathon, his race against death.

What he didn't know then was that some of the recommendations made by his physicians were futile attempts at prolonging the inevitable. Maybe they saw my father as an excellent candidate for experimental drugs because of his physical and spiritual strength. Maybe his physicians were urged on to prolong his life, even at the cost of greater suffering on Dad's part, because of the community hero status that he had acquired.

Whatever their reasons, a year after the surgery, Dad's body was buckling under the weight of the hero's burden he'd been carrying most of his adult life. He suffered anxiety, hot flashes, weight loss, fever, chills, infections, depression, panic attacks, nausea, extreme confusion, and a severe allergic reaction to one of the chemotherapy drugs.

"Page the Doctor!"

On one of my visits from Memphis, I drove Mom and Dad to the oncologist's office for his first chemotherapy treatment. The nurses greeted us with an air of hopeful enthusiasm. Once the blood work was done and Dad was set up in his recliner chair, the first round of Taxol began to drip into his veins from the bag hanging above his head. Mom and I pulled up chairs to keep him company, but in less than a minute Dad's face turned bright red and he began gasping for air. The room quickly filled with medical personnel and I heard someone say, "Page the doctor!" They unhooked the IV, administered oxygen and gave him an injection of some sort. Color returned to his face and we all began to breathe again, as if all the air had left the room and returned just as suddenly.

"Taxol is a fairly new drug," the doctor explained when he arrived. "We were hoping for a breakthrough, but Bill had a rare allergic reaction to it, so we're going to use Carboplatin and Navelbine."

That was in August of 1997. He received four full months of this cocktail. The physician's notes from a follow-up visit in January of 1998 reported that "his tolerance for this was good." But the notes also revealed that Dad had anxiety and hot flashes, and was seen in the emergency room in October for fever and chills. A large nodule in the left lung was thought to be pneumonia, and a splattering of small nodules was also present. The radiologist "thought there were more small nodules in the left lung than before and that some of these had increased in size." But the oncologist reviewed the CT scans and noted that they were performed at different intervals, which could have accounted for an appearance of growth in size.

It was difficult to get straight answers, and I often felt, during this time, that the oncologist wasn't completely transparent with my parents. But I was 200 miles away, and my parents were intelligent and capable of asking questions themselves. *Weren't they?* Years later, as I read the following paragraph near the end of the doctor's notes from that January visit, I regretted that I had not been more involved in the early stages of Dad's treatment:

"I discussed these findings with Mr. and Mrs. Johnson today. I told them that I did not think that we needed to intervene at this time. If this is metastatic disease, then subsequent follow-up will be able to verify this. These lesions are too small to biopsy now. Clinically he is doing well and does not have symptoms to suggest progression."

If this is metastatic disease? The first paragraph of the report stated that the surgery done the previous May revealed "intrapulmonary metastatic disease." *Wasn't that the reason for the four tortuous months of chemotherapy?* The notes did not indicate that any end-of-life discussion took place with my parents on that visit. Instead, they mentioned TB skin tests, steroid therapy and testosterone shots. While I was grateful that the physician had seemed to be treating Dad's physical condition as a whole, I was disturbed by his apparent lack of directness concerning Dad's prognosis. Mom and Dad seemed to have been left to their own intuition. At some point Dad expressed regret for having gone through the chemotherapy, saying that the "cure"—which was not really a cure—was worse than the disease. He wondered what the quality of the final year of his life might have been like had he chosen a different path. What if he had been counseled differently about his options? What if he had not allowed his body to be shot through with poisonous chemicals all those months? But it was too late for "what ifs." It was time to face the inevitable.

End-of-Life Preparations

Mom was Dad's primary caregiver, with help from friends and neighbors who took turns staying with Dad while Mom ran errands or took a much-needed break for herself from time to time. At some point during those fourteen months, on one of my frequent visits from Memphis, the three of us sat down to talk about end-of-life issues. Mom and I went to the funeral home to make all the arrangements, and Dad made his wishes clear to us in his Durable Power of Attorney for Health Care. He wanted no "extreme measures" near the end. He wanted to die at home, with help from hospice staff. My parents didn't show their emotions very often, but on that day, Dad could barely say the words aloud without choking up, and Mom and I were swallowing our tears as we held our caregivers' smiles intact.

I was so glad when Dad decided to quit chemo. The physical race was over. It was time to gather emotional and spiritual resources for the most important and difficult leg of the marathon. It was time to get over the wall. What the three of us shared during the final week of my father's life was the best and worst that we can know in this life. We labored through the days and suffered through the nights, touching heaven and earth simultaneously.

I watched my parents' marriage of forty-nine years turn on its head under the stress of my father's impending death. With all the distractions removed—business, running, travel, civic and social engagements—they were left face to face with their brokenness. Fortunately, they had soft hearts, a strong faith, and an enduring love. I watched as their frustration and anger leaked out. Then I watched with admiration at the reconciliation and forgiveness that followed those moments of raw truth and emotion. One night I went into the living room and found them holding hands and crying.

"What's wrong?"

Dad managed a weak smile. "Your mother has been such an

angel all these months, and I haven't been an easy patient. I've been irritable and hard to please, and it finally got to her."

I looked at Mother as she wiped her eyes and blew her nose while getting up to find more tissues.

"Mother?"

"Oh, he hasn't been a bad patient. I'm just tired is all."

But Dad wanted me to understand. "I've asked her to forgive me and she feels guilty, but she's only human. If the tables had been turned and she had been the one who was sick, I could never have taken this good care of her."

It was more emotional intimacy than I had ever seen them share in my forty-seven years as their daughter. My tears mingled with theirs as the three of us held hands and prayed together. As I returned to Memphis from that visit, I had a sense that the end was near, and it was hard to leave them.

They met with the hospice social worker the following week, and she helped them get set up with a hospital bed, portable toilet, and other supplies they would need. She shared with them the hospice philosophy for end-of-life care, and left them a booklet to read, which Mom shared with me when I returned to Jackson for what would be the final week of Dad's life. The literature was excellent. We learned that hospice is a philosophy of care with a completely different approach than most of the cure-focused healthcare system. The hospice philosophy embraces death as a natural part of living, instead of something to always fight against. It's all about comfort and pain relief for the dying, and doesn't seek to either prolong life or hasten death. I was better able to wrap my head around the concept of "letting go" than Mom was, so she took a step back and asked me to take over as primary caregiver for those final days.

Fed by Angels

I think one of the most difficult things for family members to accept—especially for a wife who has been cooking for her husband for almost fifty years—is the patient's decreasing appetite. What southern woman, or any woman for that matter, doesn't associate cooking and feeding with nurturing and loving? So, when Dad began to refuse to eat, I reminded Mom what the social worker had told us, that he was being fed by the angels as he moved away from earth and towards heaven. He no longer needed earthly food, and his transition from earth to heaven would go more smoothly if we would embrace the process and not hold onto him too tightly. As the cancer began to shut down his vital organs, it was difficult for him to even swallow the tiny bites of applesauce into which I mixed his morphine tablets after grinding them with the back of a spoon.

Lung cancer is a relentless monster that literally sucks the air from its victim's world, resulting in a feeling of perpetual suffocation that rivals the pain of the worst forms of bone cancer. Dad's body fought the monster with more vigor than most of its victims because he was a trained marathon runner. His heart was so strong that it literally refused to stop beating, for days and perhaps months after a less conditioned organ would have given up. The irony of his condition was a cause of spiritual and moral confusion for Dad. *He had done all the right things*— he had quit smoking, embraced a lifestyle of low-fat foods and running over fifty miles most weeks, and had continued to be a leader at his church and in the community. For the first time in his life, he was angry with God. He wrestled as Jacob had with the angel, until he finally allowed himself to collapse into God's arms. I witnessed this struggle with reverence, and with thankfulness for the time he had been given to prepare to meet the God he had loved and served for sixty-eight years.

Friends from the running community visited less often as they witnessed his decline. Their hero had been reduced to an invalid in diapers, and it was more than they could bear to see. Elders from his church came on Sunday nights to anoint him with oil and to pray for his healing. When no apparent miracle arrived, their visits also decreased. When a colleague from Dad's former business firm and his wife came to visit, just a few days before Dad's death, they broke down in tears at the sight of this fallen giant of their community. I had been especially close to this couple, having babysat for their children many years earlier, and so I encouraged them to spend some time talking with Dad. They shook their heads and apologized. They just couldn't do it.

My brother had been estranged from our family for many years, but as it became obvious that Dad had only a few days to live, we summoned him for a reconciliatory visit. As he asked for forgiveness and was received into his father's embrace, images of the Prodigal Son flooded my heart. Here was yet another reason to be thankful for this time of preparation, as painful as it was for Dad, and for all of us. We might think we would prefer a sudden death and the avoidance of suffering, but suffering offers opportunities for redemption. Hospice care provides the venue. It's up to the dying and their loved ones to take advantage of this unique setting.

As Dad's anxiety increased, he found it insufferable to lie in bed. He wanted to get up and walk around, which took great physical support from his caregivers. Mom and I hired sitters to relieve us from 11 p.m. to 7 a.m. so that we could sleep, but my ears were so tuned to Dad's voice that I often found myself running down the hall in the middle of the night, afraid that I would miss his passing. One night, after we had helped Dad get up and take a few labored steps—his arms around each of our shoulders for support—we put him back in the hospital bed, only to have him ask to get up again immediately. He was over six feet tall, and although he was a mere shadow of his former self, my back was screaming with pain and my emotions were raw and sleep-deprived. After hours of these repetitive transports from bed to floor and back to bed, my strength failed. I crawled onto the bed beside him and physically restrained him with my arm. I cried. I sang to him. I prayed aloud. I played his favorite music on a tape recorder we had set up beside his bed. But he cried out with all the strength he had left, "Please let me up. I can't breathe."

I asked if he wanted me to give him more morphine so that he could sleep and he whispered, "yes."

"You might not wake up if I do this, Dad. You might not be able to talk with us any more. Are you ready for that?"

His answer was clear. "Yes."

A New Physician

It was early morning and I called the hospice nurse to ask for permission to increase the morphine dose. She said she would have to ask the doctor. It seemed like an eternity before she called back with the news: the doctor wouldn't allow the dose to be increased. He said he would come by later that day to see Dad first. *Later that day?* The nurse understood my urgency and candidly encouraged me to find another physician to sign the orders, saying that Dad's physician had a reputation for not cooperating with hospice nurses.

First I called the current doctor, who validated what the nurse had told me. He would not allow the hospice nurses the authority to increase medications as needed. "They are only nurses. They are not physicians."

"But they are the ones who are here with us," I protested. "They are the ones taking care of my father! You don't know what it's like. You don't see how he is suffering. You are not *here!*"

In that moment I was no longer the child. I became the adult my parents needed me to be. I fired the doctor over the phone, called another doctor—a dear friend from my parents' church, who had also seen Dad in his pulmonary practice during the past three years—and asked him to sign the paperwork, allowing the hospice nurse to increase Dad's meds. He took care of it immediately, and the hospice nurse called and said for me to increase the morphine. The doctor also said he would drop by to see Dad in an hour or two, which he did.

At this point you might be thinking, what prevented me from making the decision to increase the dose on my own? I thought about it, more than once. No one would have known, and I could have spared myself—and more importantly, my father—several more hours of suffering. But it wasn't that simple.

I was torn between the immediacy of Dad's discomfort and the moral implications of my actions. Mom had pretty much checked out, emotionally, by that point, so I was alone with the decision. Even with the new doctor's orders to increase the morphine, I was plagued with guilt and ambivalence. Would I be shortening my father's life?

Palliative Sedation

The literature wasn't clear on this issue. Eleven years later a front-page article in *The New York Times* (December 27, 2009) chronicled the ethical, medical and emotional struggles of several terminally ill patients and their family members. "Hard Choice for a More Comfortable Death: Drug-Induced Sleep," by Anemona Hartocollis, introduced terminology like "terminal sedation" and "palliative sedation" to the general public. One of the physicians Hartocollis interviewed, Dr. Edward Halbridge, medical director at Franklin Hospital in Valley Stream on Long Island, was asked whether the meds that rendered his 88-year-old patient unconscious might have accelerated his death. "I don't know. He could have just been ready at that time."

Another physician, Dr. Lauren Shaiova, chairman of pain medicine and palliative care at Metropolitan Hospital Center in East Harlem, had drafted a twenty-page document with guidelines for palliative sedation. Seeking even more clarity in an area ridden with ambiguity, Dr. Paul Rousseau contributed an editorial to the *Journal of Palliative Medicine* in 2003—while he was a geriatrician with Veterans Affairs in Phoenix, Arizona—calling for more systematic research and guidelines. His work noted different degrees of palliative sedation, including a level termed "intermittent deep sleep."

Hartocollis' article referenced several more physicians and

spotlighted numerous personal stories to illustrate the complex issues at stake. A capstone, for me, was learning that in 2008, the American Medical Association issued a statement of support for palliative sedation, after the American Academy of Hospice and Palliative Medicine condoned "palliative sedation to unconsciousness."

As I read this comprehensive article in the midst of penning the story of my father's death many years later, I wondered if the decision I made in July of 1998 would have been any easier—or different—had this information been available at the time. Left alone with only my conscience as my guide, I made two phone calls.

First, I called my husband—an internal medicine physician who also happens to be an ordained Orthodox (Christian) priest. And then I phoned my pastor in Memphis. Neither of them could—or *would*—tell me what to do. I think they both sensed that there might not be a "right thing" to do in this situation. And so the two men whose love and wisdom I trusted most in the world were silent. Somehow I found the strength to push through the silence. I hung up the phone, asked God for mercy, and walked into the kitchen to prepare what would probably be the last dose of medicine my father would be able to swallow.

Mother went to her room, postponing the reality as long as possible, I think. Worried that Dad wouldn't be able to swallow the larger dose, I used as little applesauce as possible, working like an artist, grinding pigments with pestle and mortar until they slid smoothly from brush to canvas. Alone with Dad in the living room, I told him that the doctor had given permission for a larger dose. He nodded. I reminded him that he might not wake up. Did he want me to get Mom? Again he nodded. First I helped with the medicine, which took two or three tries before he finished the full dose. And then I wiped his mouth gently and walked down the hall to Mother's bedroom.

We returned together, and I witnessed my parents' final conversation in this life. A few minutes later, Dad closed his eyes and went to sleep.

The hospice nurse came by later, as did the physician, and each of them assured me that Dad was resting peacefully and was not in any distress. My instructions were, "If he wakes again, give him another dose of the morphine."

When the sitter arrived for the night shift, Dad hadn't moved, but his breathing was steady, so Mom and I opted for a few hours of sleep. Early the next morning the sitter knocked on the door to the room where I was sleeping. "Mrs. Cushman, I think you and your mother should come be with him now."

The Finish Line

I flew out of bed, pausing briefly to call to Mom through the open door of her room, and she followed me quickly into the living room. Once we were at Dad's side, the sitter slipped quietly into the kitchen, allowing us privacy with Dad. Her hospice training had taught her that the ragged breaths he was drawing were signs that the end was near. We had read in the hospice literature that sometimes a dying person experiences a final surge of alertness and energy, just before the end, and we didn't want to miss it. As we stood, and later sat, on either side of his bed, he slept through much of his final morning. And then it happened.

Early on the afternoon of July 9, Dad woke briefly from his coma-like sleep, smiled, and made eye contact with Mom and me for the first time in twenty-four hours.

"I love you, Daddy."

Mother could barely find her voice. "I love you, sweetie."

"It's okay, Dad. I'll take care of Mother. You can go now."

He responded to our words by squeezing our hands. And then he was gone—the most powerful sunset I have ever seen.

As we stood there holding his hands, I was struck by the

complexity of my grief, which was infused with an uneasy mixture of relief and exhaustion. But then my mother's pain, which she had contained for fourteen months, poured from her mouth like the sounds of a woman in childbirth as she collapsed onto Dad's chest. I ran around to her side of the bed to support her, and we stood there for a long time, weeping. Finally I reached for my little red Orthodox prayer book and began to read the Prayer at the Death of a Parent. Mother regained her strength and joined me as we read together the Prayer at the Death of a Spouse. And then we read the 23rd Psalm, which was Dad's favorite. I had visions of him running past the twenty-mile marker as we read the fourth verse: "And yea though I walk through the valley of the shadow of death, I will fear no evil." He had made it over the wall.

Friends

We believed in angels. And ghosts. And all things magical in this infinite universe. Sometimes we'd lie on our backs and wish on shooting stars, putting our hopes in the great unknown. Sometimes, while gazing at the heavens and dreaming of distant futures, we'd swear we'd seen a UFO. Nothing could change our minds. After all, we had each other as witnesses. That was our story, and we were sticking to it.

—Julie Cantrell, "Not All Angels Have Wings"

The Power of Three

Claire Fullerton

She was an artist, and she was dying. Diagnosed with pancreatic cancer, her name was Sooki Raphael, and she was lovely. I didn't know her well. Sooki was a friend of a friend named Georgienne Bradley, a blonde-haired biologist who started a nonprofit organization called Sea Save, whose mission of saving the world's oceans and everything in them is no small endeavor.

Georgienne has a knack for assembling friends she thinks should know one another. Her thought is when like souls meet, anything can and does happen. I met Sooki at one of Georgienne' s beachside gatherings in Malibu. I remember the exact moment Sooki touched my arm and said she loved the coat I was wearing. It was an intimate gesture that stayed with me. It's life that makes the best stories.

It's unreal to think of it, now. I'd scarcely gone anywhere in months because of the pandemic, so when Georgienne called me on a Saturday morning to ask if I wanted to make the forty-five-minute drive to Bergamot Station in Santa Monica for an art exhibit, it took me a minute to get my mind around something that seemed rather frivolous. I had to recalibrate my thinking to the idea of emerging from my isolation to the glare of the real world. At first, I hesitated. My mind wrote a list of worries, chief among them my reluctance to be in a crowd.

"It's Sooki's show," Georgienne said. "You remember Sooki."

I did remember Sooki. She was poised and soft-spoken; an

olive-toned, slip of a woman with shining brown eyes and a humble reserve. She was a Renaissance woman with a fascinating life, and rarely shared she was Tom Hanks' assistant.

"Say yes," Georgienne said. "Meet me at my house at three-thirty."

What you have to know about Georgienne is she takes Denali everywhere, including airplanes and boats. Her pure-white, Swiss German shepherd is more well-mannered than most. She's Georgienne's constant companion, her faithful service dog with the license and red vest to prove it. Denali has the uncanny ability to turn invisible. I completely forgot she was in the back seat of Georgienne's cherry-red Camaro as we navigated the Pacific Coast Highway, the beach to our right, the hills to our left, while Georgienne brought me up to speed on Sooki's prognosis.

It seemed time was tight for Sooki. Georgienne was emotional but factual, and then the subject broadened. All the way down to Bergamot Station, Georgienne and I waxed expansively on life, on death, on friendship, on what does and does not have intrinsic meaning this side of heaven. It was stream of consciousness banter, and I marveled at how easy it was to examine such things uncensored. I kept thinking the gift of friendship is the fearless latitude to compare notes with no judgment. Nobody's right or wrong in the freedom to explore the unknowable. As I rode shotgun it occurred to me that sometimes you don't know what you believe until you hear yourself say it. On the road to Santa Monica, pondering Sooki's path ahead brought much into focus.

Georgienne's cellphone rang. She put the caller on speaker. I thought my ears deceived me when a voice with Southern inflections sang through it.

"We're lost," the voice said. "Where's the entrance?"

Georgienne glanced at me and said, "Can you look up Bergamot Station on your cellphone?"

I tried. I really did, but you have to understand they tucked Bergamot Station's five-acre, campus-like structure of twenty-some-odd art galleries on Michigan Avenue, which you can't access from the Santa Monica Freeway. You have to drive a series of one-way streets taking endless left turns in what seems a maze within a larger labyrinth. Georgienne told the voice on the phone we were as lost as they were, and if any of us ever found Michigan Avenue, we'd see each other there. It took repeated attempts of retracing what felt like an exercise in futility. When we finally found Bergamot Station's gated entrance, it was by accident. And all the while, Denali kept quiet.

You don't have to be a writer to appreciate what happened next, and any reader will understand the impact. "There they are, they made it," Georgienne said, gesturing to the SUV parking behind us. Two women closed the car's doors and walked toward us.

I'll digress here to say I'm a transplanted Southerner living in Southern California. Thirty years on, and I'm not easily moved by celebrity status. But all that went by the wayside when Georgienne introduced me to the author, Ann Patchett, who came bounding up to me saying, "You're from Memphis? I'm from Nashville." And never let it be said lighting doesn't strike twice, because the woman with Ann Patchett was the singer, Patty Smyth. Let's just say this pair covered all levels of anything I've ever cared about. I was star-struck but played it cool.

I walked beside them into the complex of grey, aluminum-side buildings, and into the Rose Gallery's A-frame structure, whose polished concrete floors were illuminated by sky-lighting. The space was utilitarian, bright, airy, and partitioned. On the painted white wall leading into the foyer, *Sooki Raphael* was scrolled boldly in stencil, and beneath it the words, *These Precious Days*, which I took to be the name of Sooki's show. I was right about that, but the title wasn't exclusive, for there, on the foyer's five-foot wooden table, sat a stack of color-printed copies of an essay published in the January 2021 edition of *Harper's Magazine*, authored by Ann Patchett. Thirteen pages front and back printed on heavy cardstock, the title of Ann's widely circulated essay was *These Precious Days*.

It started to come together. I picked up the essay's copy and leafed through it. It was Ann Patchett's first person account of events that led to my standing in the gallery among a hundred or more mask-wearing patrons, who'd come to honor Sooki Raphael at her first art exhibit. Ann Patchett, Patti Smyth, and Georgienne Bradley had acted as tri-focal triage for weeks to ensure Sooki was well enough to appear and be publically knighted as an artist. And there Sooki stood, in the middle of her dream come true.

The walls vibrated with Sooki's art, and oh, her penchant with color: deep, uniquely rich, cheery, and optimistic. The forty or so paintings verged on whimsy reined in by clean lines. Owls, and poppy fields, a saxophone player, cottage scenes, beach scenes, a couple of self-portraits beside an endearing depiction of a child reading a book. Against a white backdrop, color exploded at eye level. People milled about hugging each other in greeting, their eyes crinkling above their requisite masks. The air was electric, the tone celebratory. Denali shadowed Georgienne everywhere. Sooki's mother sat in a chair in the corner, and in the middle of it all stood Sooki, lithe and elegant, receiving her guests, humble and delicate as a sparrow in a black flowered coat, while her self-appointed guardians worked the perimeter. I'd never seen such a unified front so seamless and undetectable, and I, as a fly on the wall, was close to tears thinking this is what friends are for.

It's not easy grabbing the attention of a crowd that size, but Ann Patchett is well versed in such matters, and she had a mission. She'd braved flying out to California from Nashville while lesser mortals hunkered at home in the throes of public fear during the pandemic. She walked to the fore of the gathering wearing a scoop-neck, blue linen dress and cleared her lady-like throat into a microphone in all her inimitable Southerness. She had the room's attention.

The first thing Ann Patchett did was acknowledge she was a Nashville fish-out-of-water in California, which I thought was funny, she being a woman of the world and a house-hold name to readers. She began by apologizing for her Southern accent, she did so hope there'd be no problem with interpretation. From all quadrants of the gallery, people rushed to be a part of the happening. Some took pictures; others took video. It was a crowd standing shoulder-to-shoulder for all the right reasons, assembled in support of Sooki Raphael because time was of the essence.

Somebody had to be Master of Ceremonies, and for Ann Patchett, that one was easy. With professional finesse, she gave Sooki an introduction that caused Sooki's face to blush and everyone's eyes to water. In the last few weeks of her life, Sooki accepted the microphone from Ann and stood before us a woman whose whole life led up to that moment.

You could have heard a pin drop in the gallery what with everyone's undivided attention. There was heartfelt poignancy in the room, a ceremonial quality to the proceedings, a sense of presence, and I got the impression Sooki wasn't one to seek the limelight—hers was the kind of demeanor that would rather support it—but these three friends of Sooki deemed it necessary to see their demure, deserving friend gifted with the spotlight. Because it mattered.

If I could choose one event that fully captures the spirit of loving intention, wrap my arms around it to have and hold as a frame of reference portraying the power of female friendship, I would choose Sooki Raphael's Santa Monica art exhibit and never forget it. To stand in witness from a position that's in it but not of it gave me a heightened sensitivity from an aerial view as I watched Ann Patchett, Patti Smyth, and Georgienne Bradley bless their friend Sookie on her way to heaven.

These Precious Days, indeed. That precious moment.

Late Email from Your Daughter Concerning You, My Friend

Cathy Smith Bowers

for Merrill Farnsworth

It hangs dead center
on my living room wall,
the painting I could not

go home without. One
of a sequence summoned
from your dreams. God-

head of a woman bursting
forth from the Tree of Life,
its fiery limbs curving up

and out and around
like the furls of a fiddle-
head fern, its trunk rooted

strange in a boxcar's
burgeoning stasis. Yesterday
I sipped wine with three

old friends, praising your
magician's sleight of hand.
Those swirling dervishes

of unbearable blues, exhumed,
it seems, from the antique hills
of Chartres, as if you alone

had unearthed those long ago
vanished hues. We did not
know, as we lifted our glasses

to the ordered messiness
of it all, that you had been
dead a week. This morning

from your daughter, an email
bearing the news. And a photo
taken on one of your final

days—you in those funny plastic
glasses, your bright face lifted
to the eclipsing sun.

Eulogy for Shadow

Claire Fullerton

The mornings without her are the worst,
in that slip of time between the dream state and the metal
glare of remembering Shadow's not there,
that she won't be eye-level to the bed as she has been for years
drawing me from my slumber, anxious to start her day.
The world was a big, joyous place according to Shadow,
I couldn't help but see it through her eyes.
Every morning she'd clamor that time was wasting
there were scents outside, clues in the yard, pinecones
on the ground
that couldn't wait another minute.
Oh, get up, get up, the world awaits with endless possibilities.
I am listless in her absence.
I do not want to rise from this bed.
There's no comfort in this house yet
I cannot bear to walk out to where she used to play.
I can't put my shoes on without remembering how the act
sent her into spinning rapture,
and there is too much space around me,
without her underfoot.
I never knew silence could affect me physically,
it starts with a ringing in my ears and

lands heavy on my heart.

If I rise now, every gesture in the rhythm of my day
will lack her,
   and every movement without purpose in this world
now grown flat.

I roll to my right and see her toys strewn around her fleece
covered bed.
   I should get up and put her bear and her balls away,
   find some place to put that pine cone
   but I can't bring myself to disrupt her last arrangement.
   I want to leave everything as Shadow placed it,
   I always marveled at the single-mindedness with which she
marked her place in the world.
   I think I will lie here until her spirit comes wet-nosed
to soothe me.
   I lack the strength to rise to a world that exists without her,
   and there will be no joy if her spirit does not come.
   I will lie here until I remember what joy is,
   I've been too long following Shadow's lead,
   I fear I've forgotten how to find it on my own.
   I am frozen in this bed with the thought of retrieving my
heart from Shadow.
   The prospect seems something I'm incapable of,
   and I'd rather lie in this pain, forever
   than place one foot to a floor where she does not lay.

She was ceaseless,
constant, beautiful, unending.
She came unquestioning, every time I called her name.
Hear now, Shadow, my voice as I call you,
here pretty girl,
baby come home.

Not All Angels Have Wings

Julie Cantrell

Not all angels have wings. That's what my childhood best friend told me at the age of fifteen, a week after learning that her leukemia was no longer in remission. Heather and I had spent eleven years as neighbors by then, sharing the kind of soul-sister bond that kept us close, even when she was three states away in Memphis, Tennessee receiving the best treatment available from St. Jude's Children's Research Hospital.

Back in Louisiana, I'd wait for updates, trying to maintain a normal teenage routine while Heather was fighting her own body to stay alive. After two years of chemotherapy, radiation, and mountains of pain that no child should ever have to climb, she was losing that battle.

Twice, my mother drove me from Louisiana to visit her. Twice, I entered that hospital with its cheerful colors and upbeat medical experts and photos of smiling children lining the walls. And twice, Heather told me her theory that not all angels have wings.

She said this one time in reference to her favorite nurse, a spunky redhead who always laughed at Heather's jokes and insisted that her "favorite patient" was going to live to fulfill her dream of becoming a nurse one day, just as she'd done after surviving her own battle with childhood cancer.

The second time, she said it about me. Referring to me as an angel? I saw that as an undeserving dose of praise, especially in light of Heather's pure spirit. Responding in the only way I knew, I deflected the compliment with humor.

Laughing off life's absurdities was a coping mechanism we'd learned young in Louisiana, where most of us develop resilience as early as we form our first words. From a very early age, Heather and I had already mastered how to *count our blessings*, *keep our head up*, and *give it all to God*. This default optimism came naturally in a culture where adults play jazz in the streets for funerals and pour strong drinks with neighbors while riding out the latest torrential storm.

Like most Louisianians, Heather and I were not born with silver spoons or easy graces. Coming from Louisiana meant we'd have to meet the darkness face forward, daring to sing hymns as it howled. These skills may seem ridiculous to those whose paths have been charmed. But how else would any of us stay sane when the flood waters rise and the hurricanes blow in and everything we love turns to ruin?

That day, I spun around near the side of Heather's electronic hospital bed and pretended to be shocked that someone had forgotten to give me wings. I played out the part, a pastime that had helped us endure many hot, humid hours of our youth. Searching dramatically for my missing angel wings and absent halo, I put my childhood acting skills to work right there between the IV poles and the *Get Well Soon* cards.

Heather laughed. And I laughed. And then, despite all my efforts not to, I cried. Because as she curled in pain between the giggles, her bald head shining beneath the fluorescent lights, I feared this might be the last time we'd laugh together.

Thank heavens, I was wrong.

Heather came home once again from Memphis, and we shared more laughter, more drama, more silly dance moves, more long talks beneath the hazy Louisiana moon. But each day, she grew weaker, until it came time for a Hail Mary.

In SEC country, where LSU football rules Saturday nights, anyone can tell you a Hail Mary pass is a last second long shot, a give-it-all-you've-got throw at the end of the game when nearly all of Tiger stadium makes the sign of the cross or looks to the heavens and dares to believe, if just for a second, that God is on our side.

The bone marrow transplant was Heather's Hail Mary pass, and those of us who loved her were holding our collective breath, praying and hoping that God was on our side.

When declared a match, her big sister made the sacrifice toss, lying back to let the doctors drill deep into her bones, remove her strong marrow, and inject it into Heather's diseased body. The risks were significant. The pain was real. But stronger than either was the love these sisters shared, both determined to save Heather's life and return to Louisiana as the united family of four they'd always been.

Surely it would work.

At sixteen, when I was told time was up and the pass had been dropped, I couldn't accept that Heather was no longer in this world with us. My faith had always been my anchor, and I had never doubted that God would save Heather. That she would come home again from the hospital, this time with her sister's marrow filling her bones, healthier blood cells swimming through her veins.

Once again, I'd been wrong.

Their family of four became a family of three, and tears flowed freely. Anyone who has ever mourned a child can tell you, an unanswered prayer in football is one thing. But when pleas to save an innocent teenager go unanswered, faith can be shaken.

This wasn't the first trauma my little soul had faced, and it certainly wouldn't be the last, but Heather's death rattled my heart in ways I had not yet known at such a tender age, and I began to question everything I knew of God and heaven and miracles and angels.

But as I grieved, I knew that through all her suffering,

through all her pain, through all her unanswered prayers, Heather had never once lost faith. In fact, some of her last words were claims to have seen Jesus at her bedside, a belief that brought me comfort when I felt swallowed by the dark vortex of loss and sorrow, heavy emotions for a high school teen to hold.

Before her death, Heather and I had shared years of lazy chats. We'd sit together for hours, talking about a bunch of nothing, first while riding our matching Sky Queen bikes or hiding out in the backyard treehouse I'd built with my brother . . . later by spending the night in the camper her parents kept parked behind their home or riding around town in the car I'd just started driving when she'd learned of her final relapse.

Secret by secret, story by story, we'd sway her grandmother's porch swing or shift her mother's shade-soaked hammock or rock my mother's front porch chairs and try to figure out the world, the meaning of life, and the mystery of boys.

We'd also try to figure out angels.

We believed in angels. And ghosts. And all things magical in this infinite universe. Sometimes we'd lie on our backs and wish on shooting stars, putting our hopes in the great unknown. Sometimes, while gazing at the heavens and dreaming of distant futures, we'd swear we'd seen a UFO. Nothing could change our minds. After all, we had each other as witnesses. That was our story, and we were sticking to it.

Our minds were open, and our hearts were too, and we were in love with the beauty and wonder of it all.

Once, her older, far more rebellious (and always supportive) sister had led us in a seance, covering her bedroom lamp with a red, silk handkerchief before unfolding a worn Ouija board and beckoning the spirits to "speak!" Ten years old, at most, we swore we'd seen a ghost that night, and on more than one occasion we credited our guardian angels for saving us from one of the countless disasters that always seemed to miss us by a *very* slim margin.

Until they didn't.

As I stood at Heather's casket, matching "best friends" charms shining gold around our necks, I wondered why her angel had dropped the ball. Why Mary hadn't been hailed. Why God would take this brave, sweet soul from our lives? Why so young? Why Heather? Why this? Why now?

As with most hard questions in life, there were no answers. None would have sufficed anyway, because no matter how I bent it, Heather was gone. And I was still here. And the unfair cruelty of that reality dragged me down deep.

In the years that would follow, I would bury more loved ones, many of them too young and too soon. And I'd watch others leave my life or make destructive choices, the kind of choices that would wreck the hearts of all who loved them.

In a particularly cruel twist of fate, Heather's parents would eventually bury their other child, the gorgeous older sister who'd rocked her way through adolescence with Farrah Fawcett feathered bangs, Sun-In highlights, hot pink lips, and miniskirts. The one we'd worshiped, especially because she had taught us all we could ever want to know about *kissin' and cussin' and skippin' school.* The one who, despite her rebel soul, had let the doctors remove her marrow, hoping it would be enough to save her only sibling's life.

In the end, that dark vortex of survivor's guilt got the best of her. She died with fentanyl-laced heroin running through her veins, leaving her parents and her young daughter with more questions. More sorrow. More grief.

Time and again, when prayers and questions go unanswered, when life delivers blows too brutal for words, when loss seems unmeasurable and unmanageable, I think of Heather's unshakeable faith, her claims of having seen Jesus near her bed in those final days, her promise that she wasn't afraid of death and that she wasn't alone in her walk toward heaven. I hear her describing the warm, golden glow and the circle of singing angels who surrounded her.

In my darkest hours, I hold tight to my friend's goodness,

her spirit, her light. Believing there is more to this story than what we yet know, and that someday, when our bodies can no longer carry us, the answers will come. As they did for Heather.

When they do, may we all be escorted gently from this world to the next. And may we make that transition as Heather did, with divine love guiding us into the light.

In the meantime, may we remember, not all passes are caught. Not all games are won. Not all prayers are answered. And not all angels have wings.

Peace be with you.

Contributors

Christa Allan

A true Southern woman who knows any cook worth her gumbo always starts with a roux, Christa Allan is an award-winning author who writes women's fiction, stories of hope and redemption. *Since You've Been Gone* is among Amazon's bestsellers. Her other novels include *A Test of Faith*, *Threads of Hope*, *Walking on Broken Glass*, *Love Finds You in New Orleans*, and *The Edge of Grace*. *All They Want for Christmas* is her first indie novella, She has been an invited author at Southern Festival of Books, Louisiana Book Festival, Grand Festival of Art and Books, and Pulpwood Queens Girlfriend Weekend, and is a speaker at several conferences throughout the year. She is a member of Women's Fiction Writers Association. Christa is the mother of five, grandmother of five, and retired after teaching twenty-five years of high school English. She and her now-retired husband have managed to stay sane, despite both being home together ALL the time. They recently moved to Madison, Mississippi with their neurotic dog and two cats.

Johnnie Bernhard

A former teacher and journalist, Johnnie Bernhard is passionate about reading and writing. Her work(s) have appeared in the following publications: *University of Michigan Graduate Studies Publications*, *Heart of Ann Arbor Magazine*, *Houston Style Magazine*, *World Oil Magazine*, *The Suburban Reporter of Houston*, *The Mississippi Press*, the international *Word Among Us*, *Southern Writers Magazine*, *The Texas Review*, *Southern Literary Review*, and the Cowbird-NPR production on small town America essays. Johnnie was chosen as a selected speaker in the 2020 TEDx Fearless Women Series. In 2021, she was named a teaching artist with Gemini Ink Writing Arts Center and the national TAP Summer Institute 2021. Her published novels are *Sisters of the Undertow, How We Came to Be, A Good Girl,* and *Hannah and Ariela.* She received "Best of the University Presses, 100 Books" by the Association of University Presses in 2021. www.johnniebernhardauthor.com

Cathy Smith Bowers

Cathy Smith Bowers, North Carolina Poet Laureate 2010—2012, was born and grew up in Lancaster, S.C. She was educated at USC-L, Winthrop University, Oxford, and the Haden Institute. Bowers' poems have appeared widely in publications such as *The Atlantic Monthly, The Georgia Review, Poetry, The Southern Review, The Kenyon Review,* and *Ploughshares.* In 2017 she was inducted into the South Carolina Author's Hall of Fame She now teaches in the Queens University low-residency MFA program and in the Haden Institute Spiritual Direction and Dream Leadership programs. Her most recent book is *The Abiding Image: Inspiration and Guidance for Beginning Writers, Readers, and Teachers of Poetry,* Press 53, 2021.

Sophy Burnham (Foreword)

Author of fifteen books, Sophy Burnham has published novels, award winning plays, journalism, nonfiction books, short stories, poetry, children's books, essays and articles. Her works are translated into 26 languages. Three of her books were *New York Times* and other bestsellers and most have literary book club recognition. She is best known for writing on mysticism, including *A Book of Angels, The Ecstatic Journey, The Path of Prayer,* and *The Treasure of Montségur.* Her latest nonfiction books are *The Art of Intuition: Cultivating Your Inner Wisdom,* and *For Writers Only* (about creativity). Her favorite award is "Daughter of Mark Twain," for her book, *The Art Crowd.*

Working closely with famed Broadway producer Roger Stevens, she served for five years as Executive Director of the

John F. Kennedy Fund for New American Plays, giving money to theaters to produce new plays and to playwrights to write them. Her play *Prometheus* (an adaptation of the Aeschylus fragment with a new conclusion) was produced at the Studio Theatre in Washington, DC. Her award-winning play *Penelope* (the story of *The Odyssey* from Penelope's point of view) was staged most recently at American University.

A frequent public speaker, she has appeared on scores of TV and radio shows including *Larry King Live, Oprah, The Today Show, Good Morning America* and *CBS Morning News*. Now retired, she no longer gives workshops around the country and the world. She lives in Washington D.C. and Northampton, Maine. She is an active member of the Cosmos Club of Washington, D. C., where she plays on the chess team. Her website is www.Sophyburnham.com. Look for her blog at www.sophywisdom.com.

Lauren Camp

Lauren Camp is the author of five books, most recently *Took House* (Tupelo Press). Honors include the Dorset Prize and finalist citations for the Arab American Book Award, Housatonic Book Award and New Mexico-Arizona Book Award. In 2018, she was a visiting scholar/poet at the Mayo Clinic, presenting her poems on dementia to physicians. Her poems have appeared in *Kenyon Review, Prairie Schooner, Witness*, and *Poet Lore*, and her work has been translated into Mandarin, Turkish, Spanish, Serbian and Arabic. www.laurencamp.com

Julie Cantrell

Julie Cantrell is a *New York Times* and *USA TODAY* bestselling author, editor, story coach, TEDx speaker, and ghostwriter whose works have earned literary acclaim across both the general and inspirational markets. Learn more and subscribe for a free monthly dose of joy and positivity: www.juliecantrell.com.

Susan Cushman (Editor)

This is Susan Cushman's fourth anthology to edit. Previous collections include *A Second Blooming: Becoming the Women We Are Meant to Be*, *Southern Writers on Writing*, and *The Pulpwood Queens Celebrate 20 Years!* She is also the author of two novels: *John and Mary Margaret* and *Cherry Bomb*; two memoirs: *Pilgrim Interrupted* and *Tangles and Plaques: A Mother and Daughter Face Alzheimer's*; and a short story collection: *Friends of the Library*. A native of Jackson, Mississippi, Susan lives in Memphis, Tennessee. You can read about all of her writing and subscribe to her blog at www.susancushman.com.

Nancy Dorman-Hickson

After almost twenty years as a features editor at *Southern Living* and *Progressive Farmer* magazines, Nancy Dorman-Hickson now freelances in Birmingham, Alabama. She co-authored *Diplomacy and Diamonds*, the best-selling memoir of Joanne King Herring, who was portrayed by Julia Roberts in the movie *Charlie Wilson's War*. The Mississippi native's in-progress memoir draws on stories from her rural childhood in the 1960s and 1970s to find answers to present-day questions about faith, loss, and living in today's divided world.

Ann Fisher-Wirth

Ann Fisher-Wirth's sixth book of poems is *The Bones of Winter Birds* (Terrapin Books, 2019). *Mississippi*, her fifth, is a poetry/photography collaboration with the photographer Maude Schuyler Clay (Wings Press, 2018). With Laura-Gray Street, Ann coedited *The Ecopoetry Anthology* (Trinity UP, 2013, third printing 2020). She is a senior fellow of The Black Earth Institute; has had residencies at The Mesa Refuge, Djerassi, Hedgebrook, and CAMAC, France; and has received numerous awards for her work, including a Mississippi Institute of Arts and Letters Poetry Award, two Mississippi Arts Council

Poetry Fellowships, a *Malahat Review* Long Poem Prize, a Rita Dove Poetry Award, and fifteen Pushcart nominations. Ann was 2017 Poet in Residence at Randolph College and has had senior Fulbrights to Switzerland and Sweden. She is Professor of English and directs the Environmental Studies program at the University of Mississippi.

Claire Fullerton

Claire Fullerton is the multiple, award-winning author of four traditionally published novels and one novella. Her work has appeared in numerous magazines including *Celtic Life International*, and *The Dead Mule School of Southern Literature*. She lives in Malibu, California.

Lisa Gornick

Lisa Gornick has too many degrees from too many universities. Trained as a psychoanalyst, she worked for many years in hospitals and private practice. As a writer, she has published stories, essays, and four novels: *The Peacock Feast, Louisa Meets Bear, Tinderbox*, and *A Private Sorcery*. She lives in Manhattan, and spends her free time watching boats on the Hudson, playing Bach on an ancient piano, making an occasional fruit cobbler for her husband, and sending her two sons more texts than they want.

Mandy Haynes

Mandy Haynes has spent hours on barstools and riding in vans listening to outrageous tales from some of the best songwriters and storytellers in Nashville, Tennessee. She traded a stressful career as a pediatric cardiac sonographer for the life of a beach bum wordsmith and now lives on Amelia Island with her three dogs, one turtle, and a grateful liver. She is a contributing writer for *Amelia Islander Magazine*, editor of *Reading Nation Magazine*, and author of *Walking the Wrong Way Home*, which was a finalist for the Tartt Fiction Award, and *Sharp as a Serpent's Tooth Eva and Other Stories*. Her latest book is a novella titled *Oliver*.

Suzanne Henley

Suzanne Henley, former English instructor, college development director, and hospice worker, is a fused glass and bead artist and a residential renovation designer and contractor. She is the author of *Bead by Bead*, a nonfiction narrative hybrid, and the cookbook *Sauce for the Goose*. Her personal essay "Beyond This Point There Be Dragons" is included in the anthology *A Second Blooming*; she is currently working on a second memoir and a revision and expansion of her cookbook. The grandparents of seven, she and her husband live in Memphis, Tennessee.

Jennifer Horne

Jennifer Horne served as the twelfth Poet Laureate of Alabama from 2017 to 2021. The author of three collections of poems, *Bottle Tree*, *Little Wanderer*, and *Borrowed Light*, she also has written a collection of short stories, *Tell the World You're a Wildflower*. She has edited or co-edited four volumes of poetry, essays, and stories. Her latest work is a biography of the writer Sara Mayfield, forthcoming from the University of Alabama Press. Her web page and blog, "A Map of the World," are at: http://jennifer-horne.blogspot.com/.

Angela Jackson-Brown

Angela Jackson-Brown is an award winning writer, poet, and playwright who teaches Creative Writing and English at Ball State University in Muncie, Indiana. She is a graduate of Troy University, Auburn University, and the Spalding low-residency MFA program in Creative Writing. She is the author of the novel *Drinking From A Bitter Cup* and has published in numerous literary journals. Angela's play, *Anna's Wings* was selected in 2016 to be a part of the IndyFringe DivaFest, and her play, *Flossie Takes a Stand*, was part of the Indiana Bicentennial Celebration at the Indiana Repertory Theatre. She also wrote and produced the play *It Is Well*, and she was the co-playwright with Ashay Thomas on a play called *Black Lives Matter (Too)*. In the spring of 2018, Angela co-wrote a musical with her colleague, Peter Davis, called *Dear Bobbie: The Musical*, that was part of the 2018 OnyxFest in Indianapolis, Indiana. Her book of poetry called *House Repairs* was published by Negative Capability Press in the fall of 2018, and in the fall of 2019 she directed and produced a play she wrote called *Still Singing Those Weary Blues*. Her new *When Stars Rain Down* was recently published by Thomas Nelson, an imprint of HarperCollins, and Angela was recently awarded by the Alabama Library Association the Alabama Authors Award in Poetry.

River Jordan

River Jordan is an established literary figure, speaker, teacher, and radio host. Her work has been featured by Publishers Weekly, Booklist, NPR's Book Talk, *Guideposts Magazine*, and the *Southern Literary Review*. She is the author of four novels and three spiritual memoirs. Jordan's stories are most frequently compared to Flannery O'Connor, Harper Lee, and William Faulkner and her novel *Saints In Limbo* was hailed as a "southern gothic masterpiece." She lives on a hill just a stone's throw from Nashville where she rocks on her porch at night watching the moon move through the sky and contemplates all manner of things simple and divine.

Averyell Kessler

Averyell Kessler is a native of Jackson, Mississippi. She welcomes homeless dogs, wandering cats, and even a family of hoot owls living the magnolia tree in her front yard. She spent ten years in marketing and publicity for her husband's national touring Broadway productions, where she learned that anything can happen backstage including fist fights, dressing room shenanigans, and arrests in the middle of a major downtown street. After retiring from the peace and quiet of a lengthy legal practice, she's taken up writing in hopes of finding additional peace and quiet. Averyell, a columnist for *The Northside Sun*, Jackson, Mississippi, has been published in *The Ponder Journal*, *Mississippi Magazine*, *Our South Magazine*, and *Episcopal Café*. Her weekly flash fiction posts are available on Averyellkessler.com. She is a wife, mother, grandmother, and now writer.

Cassandra King

Cassandra King is an award-winning author of five bestselling novels and two nonfiction books in addition to numerous short stories, essays, and magazine articles. Her latest book, *Tell Me A Story*, a memoir about life with hser late husband, Pat Conroy, was named SIBA's 2020 non-fiction Book of the Year. A native of LA (Lower Alabama), Cassandra resides in Beaufort, South Carolina, where she is honorary chair of the Pat Conroy Literary Center.

Sonja Livingston

Sonja Livingston is the author of four books of nonfiction, including, her latest, *The Virgin of Prince Street*, which uses an unexpected return to her childhood church to explore larger changes in ritual, religion and devotion. Her first book. *Ghostbread*, won an AWP Book Prize for Nonfiction and has been widely adopted for classroom use. Sonja's writing has been honored with a New York State Arts Fellowship, an *Iowa Review* Award, a VanderMey Nonfiction Prize, an *Arts & Letters* Essay Prize, as well as grants from Vermont Studio Center and The Deming Fund for Women. Her essays appear in many journals and are widely anthologized. Sonja is an associate professor of creative writing at Virginia Commonwealth University.

Nancy Anne Mardis

Nancy Anne Mardis works primarily in watercolor and pen and ink, sometimes doing acrylics and 3-D. Her subjects range from weddings to portraits to landscapes/houses, and, of course, angels. Her watercolor, "Rainbow Angel," is used on the cover of this collection. Associate Professor Emeritus of Business Legal Studies and Finance at the University of Memphis, she retired after 34 years in 2021 to focus on her art. She lives in Midtown Memphis.

Frederica Mathewes-Green

Frederica Mathewes-Green is a wide-ranging author who has published ten books and 800 essays, in such diverse publications as the *Washington Post, Christianity Today, Smithsonian,* and the *Wall Street Journal.* She has been a regular commentator for National Public Radio (NPR), a columnist for the Religion News Service, Beliefnet.com, and *Christianity Today,* and a podcaster for Ancient Faith Radio. (She was also a consultant for *Veggie Tales.*) She has appeared as a speaker over 600 times, at places like Yale, Harvard, Princeton, Wellesley, Cornell, Calvin, Baylor, and Westmont, and received a Doctor of Letters (honorary) from King University. She has been interviewed over 700 times, on venues like PrimeTime Live, the 700 Club, NPR, PBS, Time, Newsweek, and the New York Times. She lives with her husband, the Rev. Gregory Mathewes-Green, in Johnson City, TN. Their three children are grown and married, and they have fifteen grandchildren.

Wendy Reed

Wendy Reed is an Emmy-winning writer and producer, whose work includes documentaries and the long-running series Bookmark with Don Noble and Discovering Alabama. She also co-launched Speaking Evolution, a multi-platform program on communicating evolution. The author of *An Accidental Memoir:*

How I Killed Someone and Other Stories (NewSouth Books) and co-editor of *All Out of Faith* and *Circling Faith* (University of Alabama Press) teaches science-writing seminars for Honor College students. She is a State Council on the Arts fellow and has been recognized by Oregon State University, The Lillian E. Smith Center, the Seaside Institute, and Lincoln University for her work. Her essays and stories have been published in newspapers, anthologies, and literary magazines. She is an MPH student and most recently has been busting her ass trying to get Alabamians vaccinated against Covid-19.

Joanna Seibert

The Rev. Joanna Seibert MD is an emeritus professor of radiology and pediatrics at Arkansas Children's Hospital and the University of Arkansas Medical Sciences and has been an ordained deacon in the Episcopal Church for twenty years. She is the author of numerous books including, *The Call of the Psalms, a Spiritual Companion for Busy people* and *The Call of the Psalms, a Spiritual Companion for People in Recovery, Healing Presence*, as well as two books of sermons, *Interpreting the World to the Church* vol. 1 and 2. Her newest books are *A Daily Spiritual Rx for Lent and Easter* and *A Daily Spiritual Rx for Advent, Christmas, and Epiphany*, and *A Daily Spiritual Rx for Ordinary Time*. Joanna had been named one of the top 100 women in Arkansas by *Arkansas Business* for several years. In 2017 she was named to the Arkansas Women's Hall of Fame. Joanna and her husband have three grown children and six grandchildren and have lived in Little Rock for forty-five years.

Sally Palmer Thomason

Sally Thomason, Ph. D., retired dean of continuing and corporate education at Rhodes College, is a lifelong student/teacher/administrator/author with an interdisciplinary approach to culture and history. She has written four books: *The Living Spirit of the Crone: Turning Aging Inside Out; The Topaz Brooch; Delta Rainbow: The Irrepressible Betty Bobo Pearson;* and *The Power of One—Sister Anne Brooks and the Tutwiler Clinic.*

Natasha Trethewey

Natasha Trethewey served two terms as the 19th Poet Laureate of the United States (2012-2014). She is the author of five collections of poetry, including *Native Guard* (2006)—for which she was awarded the 2007 Pulitzer Prize—and, most recently, *Monument: Poems New and Selected* (2018); a book of non-fiction, *Beyond Katrina: A Meditation on the Mississippi Gulf Coast* (2010); and a memoir, *Memorial Drive* (2020) an instant *New York Times* Bestseller. She is the recipient of fellowships from the Academy of American Poets, the National Endowment for the Arts, the Guggenheim Foundation, the Rockefeller Foundation, the Beinecke Library at Yale, and the Radcliffe Institute for Advanced Study at Harvard. She is a fellow of both the American Academy of Arts and Sciences and the American Academy of Arts and Letters. In 2017 she received the Heinz Award for Arts and Humanities. A Chancellor of the Academy of American Poets since 2019, Trethewey was awarded the 2020 Rebekah Johnson Bobbitt Prize in Poetry for Lifetime Achievement from the Library of Congress. Currently, she is Board of Trustees Professor of English at Northwestern University.

Jacqueline Allen Trimble

Jacqueline Allen Trimble is a National Endowment for the Arts Creative Writing Fellow (Poetry), a Cave Canem Fellow and an Alabama State Council on the Arts Literary Fellow. Her work has appeared in various journals, including *Poetry Magazine, The Louisville Review, The Offing*, and *Poet Lore*, the anthology *The Night's Magician* (Negative Capability Press), a collection of eighty poems by contemporary writers on the moon, and *Southern Writers on Writing* (University Press of Mississippi), an anthology of twenty-six essays by Southern writers. Published by NewSouth Books, *American Happiness*, her debut collection, won the 2016 Balcones Poetry Prize. She lives and writes in Montgomery, Alabama, where she is Professor of English and chairs the Department of Languages and Literatures at Alabama State University. Her new collection, *How to Survive the Apocalypse*, is forthcoming from NewSouth Books in April 2022.

Renea Winchester

Renea Winchester is a first-place winner of the North Carolina Press Association Award, the recipient of the Wilma Dykeman Award for Essay, and a two-time winner of the Appalachian Writer's Award. In April 2020, Firefly Southern Fiction released Renea's debut novel, *Outbound Train*. Set in her hometown of Bryson City, North Carolina, *Outbound Train* won the Blue Ridge Writers Award in 2021, and was nominated for the Crook's Corner Prize, and was a finalist for Best New Fiction (American Book Fest). In April 2021, *Outbound Train* was translated into French and released internationally with a new title, *De l'autre Cote' des rails*. In May, the Nova Aquitaine Independent Booksellers chose *Rails* as a France summer read. Renea is the author of several non-fiction works including *Farming, Friends & Fried Bologna Sandwiches* (Mercer University Press) which was nominated for the prestigious SIBA award and earned Renea a nomination for Georgia Author of the Year. Renea has served on the Atlanta Writers Board, Georgia Writers Association, and judges multiple literary awards. Renea is currently working on her next novel, *The Mountains Remember*, a historical novel based on her grandmother's displacement to form the Great Smoky Mountains National Park. As a descendant of those who were displaced, Renea is passionate about Appalachian Heritage, preserving rare seeds, cultivating endangered plants, and meeting new friends.

Permissions

- Christa Allan: Published by permission of the author.
- Johnnie Bernhard: Published by permission of the author.
- Cathy Smith Bowers: Published by permission of the author.
- Sophy Burnham: Published by permission of the author.
- Lauren Camp: "A Precise Small Thing," originally published in *This Business of Wisdom*, West End Press, 2010. Reprinted with permission from the author.
- Lauren Camp: "Goodbye to Aggressions and Generous Gestures," originally published in *Epiphany*, January, 2020. Reprinted with permission from the author.
- Lauren Camp: "Prayer For My Father's Frontal Lobes," originally published in *Spry Literary Journal*, October 2016. Reprinted with permission from the author.
- Julie Cantrell: Published by permission of the author.
- Susan Cushman: Published by permission of the author.
- Nancy Dorman-Hickson: Published by permission of the author.
- Ann Fisher-Wirth: "And Behind Us, Only Air," originally published in Quartet Journal, 2021. Reprinted with permission from the author.
- Ann Fisher-Wirth: "Inhabitation," originally published in *Persimmon Tree*, 2021. Reprinted with permission from the author.
- Ann Fisher-Wirth: "Persimmons," originally published in *Shenandoah*, 2022. Reprinted with permission from the author.
- Ann Fisher-Wirth: "Thum," originally published in *Eco Theo Review*, 2021. Reprinted with permission from the author.
- Claire Fullerton: Published by permission of the author.
- Lisa Gornick: "The End," originally published in *Salon*, March 12, 2016. Reprinted with permission from the author.
- Mandy Haynes: Published by permission of the author.

About the Editor

Susan Cushman is author of five books—two novels, two memoirs (most recently *Pilgrim Interrupted*), and a short story collection, and editor of three previous anthologies, including *Southern Writers on Writing*. A native of Jackson, Mississippi, Susan lives in Memphis with her husband of 53 years. They are both converts from the Presbyterian Church to the Orthodox Church. She has three grown children and four grandchildren. Susan has not yet seen angels in person, but she has a growing relationship with her guardian angel, who has been with her in at least two near-death experiences.